אשא עיני

VISIONS
of HOLINESS
in the EVERYDAY

NINA BETH CARDIN

EDITED BY ARI Y. GOLDBERG

United Synagogue of Conservative Judaism • Depar[...]

UNITED SYNAGOGUE OF CONSERVATIVE JUDAISM DEPARTMENT OF YOUTH ACTIVITIES

Jules A. Gutin, *Director*
Gila R. Hadani, *Assistant Director*
Ari Y. Goldberg, *Assistant Director for Education*
Marsha B. Goldwasser, *Activities Coordinator*
Nadine R. Greenfield, *Projects Coordinator*
Marc Louis Stober, *Publications Coordinator*
Ze'ev Kainan, *Central Shaliach*
Yitzchak Jacobsen, *Director, Israel Office*
David Keren, *Nativ Director*

CENTRAL YOUTH COMMISSION

Marshall Baltuch, *Chairman*
Jonathan S. Greenberg, *Education Committee Chairman*

UNITED SYNAGOGUE OF CONSERVATIVE JUDAISM

Stephen S. Wolnek, *President*
Rabbi Jerome M. Epstein, *Executive Vice-President*

A publication of the National Youth Commission,
United Synagogue of Conservative Judaism
155 Fifth Avenue, New York, New York 10010
First Edition, 1997

Manufactured in the United States of America.

Guide to Hebrew Names for Books of the Bible

Bereshit = Genesis

Shemot = Exodus

Vayikra = Leviticus

Bamidbar = Numbers

Devarim = Deuteronomy

Shoftim = Judges

Shmuel = Samuel

Melakhim = Kings

Tehillim = Psalms

Mishlei = Proverbs

Shir HaShirim = Song of Songs

Eikhah = Lamentations

Kohelet = Ecclesiastes

Divrei HaYamim = Chronicles

Table of Contents

Editor's Preface

Over the years USY has produced sourcebooks on a wide variety of topics, ranging from the rituals of Kashrut and Shabbat, the philosophy of the Conservative Movement, and the history of Jerusalem and Zionism, to name just a few. However, this year's sourcebook may be one of the most important because it goes to the very heart and essence of Judaism. What is Judaism if we don't love it, celebrate it, and cherish it? Toward that end, this sourcebook will give the reader the tools to see the "visions of holiness in the everyday." By being able to see these visions of holiness, our lives and our souls will be enriched.

The Hebrew title of this book is אֶשָּׂא עֵינַי. Translated as "I will lift my eyes," אֶשָּׂא עֵינַי are the opening two words of Psalm 121. This Psalm conveys this sourcebook's goal of striving to help the reader to find God and holiness in the world around us.

> *I will lift my eyes to the hills*
> *From where comes my help.*
> *My help comes from the Lord*
> *Who made heaven and earth* (Tehillim 121:1-2)

USY is very fortunate to have had Rabbi Nina Beth Cardin author this sourcebook. She has produced a book replete with sources, both historic and modern, as well as presenting the information via a uniquely prosaic writing style which only enhances the book's ability to help us to see the "visions of holiness in the everyday."

We are very grateful to a talented group of readers who played a very important role in shaping this book, especially in terms of the exercises and marginal comments.

Jacob Blumenthal
Rabbi Diane Cohen
Rabbi Jerome M. Epstein
Jonathan S. Greenberg
Jack Gruenberg
Jules A. Gutin
Gila R. Hadani
Rabbi Shira Leibowitz

As you read this book you will see that it contains a distinctive layout. On the outside margin of each page of text is a box which contains supplementary comments to the main part of the sourcebook. These marginal comments follow a standard style throughout the book in order to assist the reader in understanding the nature of the comment. **Questions for reflection appear bold, like this.** Additional comments from the author appear in regular typeface, like this. *Statements from the readers which bring another viewpoint about the points being discussed appear in italics, like this. Initials following these comments refer to the readers above.* Finally, comments with only a word or phrase in **bold** refer to a matching term in the text and serve as a definition or further explanation of that word or phrase.

Throughout the book, you will notice the following symbol followed by a double underlined number. [e.g. ☞<u>22</u>] This indicates that there is an exercise at the end of the chapter which relates to this section of the text. In this case, the related exercise is on page 22.

I must thank my wife, Stacy, for her continued love and support and to my daughter Rina, whose daily exploration of the world around her facilitates my ability to see visions of holiness in the everyday.

Ari Y. Goldberg
October 1997

Introduction

We are a generation searching for our way. How odd, for we are a generation that knows more now than at any other time in human history. We have peered inside the atom and across the universe. A flood of facts pours every day out of our laboratories, think tanks, research groups, scholars' minds, and stock markets, and into the world around us. A modem lets us ride the wave.

But knowledge does not itself yield meaning, and facts alone do not equal truth. The most sophisticated microscopes in the world cannot help us see why we are here. And the most powerful telescopes cannot pinpoint the source of holiness. Yet meaning and holiness are what we need to guide our lives. They help us choose to do the things that together pile up to form the stuff of our lives. They help us answer: what shall I do today? How shall I respond to the opportunities and demands that come my way? How do I know what is right? What should I do when I make a mistake? What will lift me when I fall?

This book is about the beliefs, stories and rituals that form the grand wisdom we call Judaism. Judaism is a compass that guides us to holiness and meaning. As a compass always points north, so Judaism always points toward God. This book attempts to lay out the various points on this compass of Judaism, the various ways we can travel in our lifelong trek toward the source of holiness.

In this book you will find many paths that Jews throughout the ages traveled in their journeys of holiness. No doubt you will respond to some approaches more powerfully than to others. You may discover that some paths preclude others. If you take this one, you cannot take that one. Other paths might appear contradictory, yet you may find that you can take them both at once. Such is the nature of this compass and the extraordinary pull of God. And that is fine. For remember, the goal is not to find the one right way, but to find your right way.

This book is laid out in classic rabbinic style, with the running narrative in the middle of the page and additional thoughts, quotes, and comments along the sides. The extra space in the margins is for you to write your responses, adding your voice to the chorus arrayed before you.

At the end of each chapter you will find exercises that help translate ideas of the chapter into your everyday life. The ideas in this book are meant to be used.

So grab the compass, bring along a friend, and have a great journey.

Nina Beth Cardin
Rosh Hodesh Heshvan 5758

Chapter 1:
Seeking God

"When we begin to speculate on a subject so vast and important [as the nature of God], we must not decide any question by the first idea that suggests itself to our minds, or force our thoughts to obtain a knowledge of the Creator too quickly, but we must wait patiently and modestly advance step by step." (Rambam, Guide to the Perplexed 1:5) ☞21

When my son was four, he went on his first airplane ride. The day before the trip, we talked about flying, and how it felt to rise high above the trees and fields and buildings, and about the marvel of looking down upon the world that only a moment before held us fast. About how it felt to ride the wind and how time seems to thicken and reform itself in the air. And then I turned to him and asked.

"Do you know what we will see when we go up in a plane?"

"Yes," he replied, his eyes widening, filling with wonder. "God," he whispered.

Well, that took me by surprise. I was thinking more along the lines of clouds. I stood for a moment in awe of my son. But what struck me even more than his faith at that moment (and my sadness at not being able to share his certainty) was his readiness, his eagerness about being on the verge of meeting God. He was positively glowing with anticipation.

How would I feel, I wondered, if I ever knew for certain that I would be meeting God, face-to-face, within 24 hours? How would you feel?

Fear was definitely one of my first emotions. How would I measure up in the presence of God? Who would judge me more harshly, God or me? By what standard would I be measured?

And yet, after a while (my son had long before moved on to other things), my feelings of fear and judgment subsided. Peace and calm settled upon me. To see God! To be in the presence of God! What could be more desirable; more comforting? This was not a summoning before a court. This was the ultimate re-union, a homecoming, a resting place.

A hasidic story tells us that before his death, Rabbi Zusya, was reported to have said, "In the coming world, they will not ask me: Why were you not Moses? They will ask me: why were you not Zusya?" What does this tell us about the standard by which we will be measured? What, according to this saying, is our life's task? What does it take to be true to oneself?

2

☞22

The term **Shekhinah** signifies the majestic presence of God among human beings. It usually implies an intimate awareness of God's company.

The **mahzor** is the prayer book which is used on Rosh Hashanah and Yom Kippur. It contains many piyutim (poems) proclaiming God's love and mercy for the Jewish people.

Consider the rabbis' view of paradise. It was the garden, the ultimate gathering place where *"the righteous sit with wreaths adorning their heads, and bask in the radiance of the **Shekhinah**." (Berakhot 17a)*. Paradise is - quite simply - the joyful awareness of being in the presence of God. Not doing, not receiving; just being.

The Hebrew poet Chayim Nahman Bialik describes the quiet power of presence in one of his poems about love, which always seemed to me one of the finest metaphors for God.

> *"Draw me close, beneath your wing;*
> *as mother, sister, when I despair;*
>
> *Your lap is a refuge for my head;*
> *a nest for my rejected prayers."*[1]

God is comforter, protector, refuge; the One who takes us in when others may have pushed us out. No questions, no chiding, no excuses, no blame. Just acceptance and peacefulness and a place to rest one's head.

Why, then, these different reactions in me: fear, anticipation, comfort, surrender? Where did they come from? What other images of God shape our relationship to the divine? ☞22

Judaism is full of rich images of God. God is depicted as creator, lawgiver, warrior, defender, mother, lover, judge, comforter, parent, refuge, deliverer, teacher, artist. All these images, and more, are found in our classic texts: Torah, N'viim (Prophets), K'tuvim (Writings), Talmud, midrash, siddur, **mahzor**. At one moment, God is our liberator from Egypt. In another, God is a friend bringing comfort to those who mourn. These images, fluid and flowing, pave the way for our rich relationships with God.

Limits of Our Images

But we should never forget that these images are cast in human form created by human language from the knowledge of human experience. These images help us approach God. They help us understand God. But they are not God. They portray God but do not contain God. We live in this paradox, then: to speak of God is to utter both a blessing and a blasphemy. To fit God into our human constructs of behavior, logic, emotions, morality, physics, and causality is to create an idol. Yet, what else can we do? Shall we say nothing and think nothing and therefore do nothing about God; or shall we speak of God and think of God and respond to God imperfectly?

Throughout human existence, people have chosen the imperfection of speech over the isolation of silence.

Judaism, of course, recognizes this imperfection of speech. Our varying and sometimes competing images of God - stern judge and compassionate friend; warrior and mother - remind us that no one image is correct, and no composite of images is correct. But they also - together - teach us not to be afraid to speak about God.

This book is designed to do just that: to help us construct our own views of God, culled from tradition's rich imagery of God, and to build our own ways of responding to these views. Such a task can take a lifetime; perhaps better said, it should take a lifetime. So this book offers a guide to Judaism's multiple paths toward God and it offers a way to map and chronicle our journeys. For every bit as important as the journey toward God, is our response to the lessons we learn on the way.

We begin with some classic images and views of God. ☞<u>23</u>

Harahaman - God as Compassionate Creator

One of our first images of God is that of creator - separate from, yet one with the world. "God is the place of the world but the world alone is not God's place," the rabbis tell us. Powerful, awesome, God creates the world, takes delight in it and tends to it:

> *At the beginning of God's creating of the heavens and the earth, when the earth was wild and waste, darkness over the face of Ocean, rushing-spirit of God hovering over the face of the waters --*
>
> *God said: Let there be light! And there was light.*
> *God saw the light: that it was good.*
> *God separated the light from the darkness.*
> *God called the light: Day! and the darkness he called: Night!*
> *There was setting, there was dawning: one day.*
> *(Bereshit 1:1-5)[2]*

God crafted the world, and assessed it by stages, day one, day two, day three, and so on, as if to continually test its soundness. Creation is more than the handiwork of God. It is the way God begins to know us, and the way we begin to know God; both the majesty and the mystery of God.

Pick the subject you know most about. Write down all the facts you can think of about that subject in thirty seconds. Then, write down all the things you don't know about that subject in thirty seconds. What does this teach you about the relative positions of humans and God in the universe?

4

God as Creator is found in both our morning and evening services:

Morning: Blessed are You, God, Ruler of the Universe, who creates light and fashions darkness, who makes peace, Creator of All. You light up the world and all who live there with mercy, and in goodness you renew - every day - the works of creation.

Evening: Blessed are You, God, Ruler of the Universe, whose word brings the evening dusk. You open the gates of time with wisdom, and change the day's divisions through understanding, set the succession of the seasons, array the stars in their paths in the skies according to your will. You create day and night, rolling light away before darkness, and darkness before light. Blessed are You, God, for each evening's dusk.

What can we imagine about God once we learn that humans are made in God's image? How does this affect the way we relate to God?

Pirkei Avot (Ethics of the Fathers) is one of the 63 tractates of the Mishnah and deals largely with ethical principles of daily living.

God's creating was not accidental or whimsical. We humans are not part of a divine game but a divine plan. God created man and woman, blessed them, and sent them into the world with a charge and a mission (much as parents do when their children come of age) saying:

> *Bear fruit and be many and fill the earth and subdue it!* (Bereshit 1:28)

God's compassion extended beyond giving humanity companionship, the capacity to learn, and a fertile world. God gave us an even greater legacy: the likeness of the Divine. It is this which allows us to bridge the gulf between the Creator and creature, between meaning and emptiness.

> *Let us make humanity in our image and in our likeness... And God created humanity in God's likeness, in the likeness of God humanity was created; male and female God created them.* (Bereshit 1:26-27)

God embedded the marker for holiness in our very genes. We have the capacity to transform our human behavior into movements of the Divine. This story of creation makes us aware of this. It continually renews our sense both of who we are, and Whose we are; what we can do and what we can be. Possessing this spark of the Divine and knowing that we possess this spark of the Divine are signs of Divine compassion.

As it states in **Pirkei Avot**: *Rabbi Akiba taught: Humanity is beloved [by God] for we are created in the image of God. But it was an even greater act of love when God told us we were created in the divine image, as it says "And God blessed Noah and his sons saying: ... In the image of God was humanity made (Bereshit 9:6)."* (Avot 3:17)

How unfortunate, and perhaps pointless, to be made in God's image and never know. It would be like being married to someone and not knowing, or like having a million dollars and no one ever telling you. It is the knowledge of our condition that motivates us to respond to it. Telling us of our potential divinity is perhaps the grandest gift of our creation.

The story of Bereshit also teaches us that God's compassion extends beyond creation. It includes the way God responds to us every day. How easy it would be for the One who is Perfect to lose patience with those who are not. Yet, God does not require us to be perfect. God simply wants us to try. Humans are, well, human. And falling short of the mark is in the nature of our being. (That, in fact, is the meaning of heit - sin: missing the mark) God recognizes this and, like a parent, lovingly reproves us when we stray, all the while encouraging us to find a better way.

Bereshit demonstrates God's compassion with a story: Adam and Eve disobeyed God, hid, and failed to take responsibility for their actions. So what did God do?

The Torah shows us that after meting out their punishment, God seeks to offer them comfort and reconciliation: *"And the Lord God made the man and the woman garments of skin, and God clothed them."* (Bereshit 3:21) After witnessing their disobedience, after declaring that they had done wrong, God seeks to reweave the frayed relationship. The garments sewn by God's hand mend the tear in intimacy caused by misdeed, judgment and punishment. Adam and Eve begin the relationship with God anew.

This view of God as Compassionate Creator, one who prods us to be our best but who supports us when we fail, is renewed every day in our morning prayer, *Barukh She'amar.* Its simple, mantra-like, cadenced language ushers in **Pesukei d'Zimra**:

Blessed is the One who Speaks and the world was! *Baruch hu!*
Blessed is the Maker of creation.
Blessed is the One whose speaking is doing.
Blessed is the One who decides and it is done.
Blessed is the One who brings forth mercy for all the earth!
Blessed is the One who brings forth mercy for all the creatures!
Blessed is the One who responds kindly to the faithful!
Blessed is the One who rolls away darkness and brings light!
Blessed is the Eternal who lives forever!
Blessed is the One who rescues and redeems. *Baruch sh'mo!*

Why is mercy mentioned twice? Because creation yields imperfection. Nothing but God is perfect. And yet, God does not give up on creation. God reaches out to creation, bringing us strength and goodness and light and redemption. And ultimately, despite all our shortcomings, God continues to desire creation. That is the ultimate act of compassion. ☞25

HaMetzaveh - God as Law Giver

Perhaps the best known image of God is that of Law Giver, the One who sets rules and expectations, the One who shows us the way we should walk through life. In fact, the first words God spoke to Adam were: *"From every tree of the garden you may eat, but from the tree of the knowledge of good and evil, you shall not eat."* (Bereshit 2:16-17) God relates to us through the giving of the commandments and we relate to God through the performance of commandments. It is this biblical view of divine call and human

"Seeking God means seeking to understand a part of ourselves that we don't see simply by looking in a mirror. We need a different mirror. The image of God reweaving the severed relationship is a wonderful example of how we can act according to God's example in our own lives." - D.C.

Pesukei d'Zimra, a medley of Psalms and other Biblical passages, precedes the main part of the Shacharit (morning) service.

6

response that defines the Jews to this very day. The rabbis translated this language into 613 commandments, so many commandments that our days are full of conversation with God.

And love of God:

> *You shall love the Lord your God with all your heart, with all your soul and with all your might. And let these words which I command you this day forever be upon your hearts. You shall teach them diligently to your children. You shall recite them while at home and away, evening and morning. You shall bind them as a sign upon your hand and they shall be a reminder above your eyes; you shall inscribe them upon the doorposts of your homes and upon your gates.* (Devarim 6:4-9)

The laws are a bridge, not a barrier, between God and the Jews. They offer us a way to meet God; a path toward God. Not love *or* law but love *and* law.

"Oh, how I love your law, your testimonies are my meditation," writes the psalmist. *"Happy are they who are upright in the way, who walk in the law of the Lord."*

For both God and the Jews, the laws are an expression of love. Abraham Joshua Heschel teaches that the Torah - the source of the law - is not the transcript of the word of God, after all, but a midrash, our human record of the revelation at Sinai. At Sinai, God promised to be our God and we promised to be God's people. This meeting, then, was a wedding. The Torah is our document that serves as our ketubah; our eternal witness and steward of this promise. Just as when we love someone we promise to do certain things for them, so too when we love God we promise to do certain things. In a way then, we humans are partners in fashioning the law.

The laws connect us with holiness: *"Blessed are you, God, Ruler of the Universe, who sanctifies us through your commandments..."* Doing what God asks of us, or what we believe God asks of us, <u>because</u> God asks it of us sanctifies that which we do. When we light candles every Friday night, for example, we transform a common task of turning back the dark into a sacred meeting with **eternity**.

Every day, as part of the Shacharit (morning service), we praise God for giving us the Torah, the source of all commandments and our knowledge of the divine: *"Blessed are you, God, Ruler of the Universe, who chose us from all the peoples of the world to give us your Torah. Blessed are you, God, who gives the Torah."*

How can law reflect love? We usually think of obeying laws to avoid punishment or safeguard social welfare. How does this concept affect your understanding?

The Rabbis call Shabbat "a taste of the world to come." When we light the Shabbat candles, we open the portal to Shabbat, and at that moment, we taste **eternity**.

Tradition speaks often of feeling God's love through the laws: *"Blessed are you God... who sanctifies us through your commandments, who desires us, and who willingly gives us the Sabbath, in love..."* *"In great love have you loved us,"* we declare before the morning Sh'ma. *"You love us with eternal love,"* we sing before the evening Sh'ma, *"teaching us your Torah and commandments, laws and statutes... We rejoice in your words, for they are our lives, and the length of our days."*

God is the one who speaks, and we respond, much as a lover seeking to do the wishes of her beloved. ☞<u>25</u>

God as Judge

<u>26</u>☜ As Creator, God judged the world. As Commanding One, God judges the world. The Torah tells us that God judged Adam and Eve, the generation of Noah, the people of Sodom and Gomorrah. Abraham was not surprised at God as Judge. He was only surprised at the way God chose to judge: *"Shall the Judge of all the earth not deal justly?" (Bereshit 18:25)*

This image of judge and justice pervades the Bible, and is found most powerfully in our High Holiday prayers. We imagine heaven as a court of justice and the synagogue as its earthly reflection. As it says at the beginning of the Kol Nidrei service, the preamble to Yom Kippur: *"By the authority of the court on high and by the authority of the court below..."* All the world that day is transformed into a courtroom.

In the Unetane tokef prayer, we proclaim God's role as judge:

> *"Your throne (seat of justice) is established in compassion, you sit upon it in truth. You judge, you witness, you prosecute. You remember all that had been forgotten; you open the records of the past. They speak for themselves, we each have signed them ourselves."*

We tremble: Is there room for compassion in such a world?

> *"On Rosh Hashanah it is written and on Yom Kippur it is sealed:*
>
> *Who shall live and who shall die; who in the fullness of their lives and who prematurely; who by fire and who by water; who by sword and who by beast; who*

God can give us rules and guidelines; God can point the way and show us what to do. But God, the great Commanding One, cannot force our response. In that moment of awareness, in that window of vulnerability, God ceases to be a distant, strict commander (if God ever was). God is revealed as a caring God (as God in truth appears throughout much of the Torah), as a God who seeks a homeland for Israel, long life and loving families for the Jewish people. The consequences of disobeying the laws seem less like punishments and more like over-zealous efforts at persuasion. (We see it in God's response to the very first transgression, the eating of the fruit. Adam and Eve did not die on that very day, because God chose to be compassionate, rather than lonely. Sodom was given a way to save itself, because God desired to turn compassion into a category of justice.)

8

by famine and who by thirst; who by earthquake and who by plague; who will rest and who will roam; who will be at peace and who shall be tormented; who will become poor and who will be rich."

This is a strict and exacting God; a God of rule and law. If we disobeyed, if we were wrong, we will be punished. And on the High Holidays, we admit by the words of our mouths and the record of our own hand that we have wronged God and each other!

"We abuse, we betray, we are cruel, we destroy, we embitter, we falsify, we hate, we insult, we jeer, we kill, we lie, we mock, we neglect, we oppress, we pervert, we quarrel, we rebel, we steal, we transgress, we are unkind, we are violent, we are wicked, we are xenophobic, we yield to evil, we are zealots for the wrong causes." (The "Ashamnu" confessional prayer recited on Yom Kippur)[3]

These are harsh judgments that we pass on ourselves. How can we live, given our frailties? How shall we escape punishment, seeing we are guilty?

But the Judge of the world is not like a human judge, and the ways of a divine court are not like the ways of a human court. Human courts are designed to verify truth and mete out justice. The divine court is designed to foster repentance and dispense compassion. God is more interested in forgiveness than retribution; in our contrition than our punishment.

"But repentance (teshuvah), prayer (tefillah) and giving (tzedakah) avert the severity of the decree."

God would much rather sit on the throne of mercy than the throne of justice. And so we beseech the God of justice on this day of justice to have mercy, to be true to the godly attributes spoken to Moses and repeated in our High Holiday liturgy: *"Adonai, Adonai, God of mercy and tenderness, patient, full of kindness, seeing the truth beyond truth..."*

To think of God as judge, then, is to know that divine justice operates differently than human justice. ☞26

Do you think that God actually judges the earth? Do you think that we see justice in the world? How is this concept of God helpful to our understanding of and relationship to God?

Considering the statement about the difference between the divine court and the human court, do you believe that human courts should behave more like the divine court?

God as Person

In the Jewish tradition, God is endowed with personality. In our stories and our prayers, God is spoken of as father, king, judge, warrior, savior, and so on. But God of course is none of these. God is not a person, and God does not possess human attributes. In truth, God exceeds the limits of our language. *"The heaven and the heaven of heavens cannot contain you, God,"* declared King Solomon when he dedicated the Holy Temple. *"How much less the house that I have built."* How much less, we might add, the language we speak.

Yet as humans facing the cosmos, in a quest for the laws, unity, love, and values that can give our lives meaning, we often choose to locate these concepts in the image of a divine "personality." This helps us focus our thinking about God, and it helps us to understand godliness better. As Jews, we choose to talk about God as a "holy person" so that we too can become a holy person.

To speak of God as personality, then, is to reflect back toward God the notion that we are made in God's image. If we are a reflection of God's image, human logic forces us to think, God is - as it were - a reflection of our image. This understandably makes profound claims on us.

The way God behaves is, to some extent, the way we should behave. This is what the rabbis teach us in the following texts:

> *"To walk in all God's ways"* (Devarim 11:22), These are the ways of the Holy One: *"gracious and compassionate, patient, abounding in kindness and faithfulness, assuring love for a thousand generations, forgiving iniquity, transgression, and sin, and granting pardon...."* (Shemot 34:6). This means that just as God is gracious and compassionate, you too must be gracious and compassionate. *"The Lord is righteous in all His ways and loving in all His deeds"* (Tehillim 145:17). As the Holy One is righteous, you too must be righteous. As the Holy One is loving, you too must be loving. (Sifre Devarim, Ekev)[4]

> *"Follow the Lord your God"* (Devarim 13:5). What does this mean? Is it possible for a mortal to follow God's Presence? The verse teaches us that we should follow the attributes of the Holy One, praised be He. As He clothes the naked, you should

10

clothe the naked. The Bible teaches that the Holy One visited the sick; so you should visit the sick. The Holy One comforted those who mourned; so you should comfort those who mourn. The Holy One buried the dead; so you should bury the dead" (Sotah 14a)[5]

God as personality comes with limitations. We can be swept away by the images we create and begin to think of God as our creation, male or female, with all our human limitations. That leads us towards blasphemy. And yet to cease to speak of God as person threatens to rob us of the intimate relationship we seek with God, and of the model of the person we strive to be.

What to do? Continue to speak of God as person, with multiple ways of being, even contradictory ways of being. That way, we get the benefit of divine intimacy without the danger of creating a vision of god in our own limited image.☞26

God as Covenantal Partner

Jewish tradition gives us rich images of our relationship with God.

> *"We are your children and you are our parent; we are your flock and you are our shepherd; we are your creation and you are creator; we are your lover and you are our Beloved; we have chosen you and you have chosen us."* (High Holiday liturgy)

All these relationships have one thing in common: they assume a covenantal relationship between the Jewish people and God. This covenantal relationship is one in which each partner is bound to the other through love, obligation, and mutual benefit. It means that each side has its role to play, and is aware of the role it is to play.☞27

It is the aspect of personality that allows us to make God our covenantal partner, and hence, a partner in our identity. God completes us. When we know ourselves as creation, we feel a bond with our Creator. When we are children, God is our parent. When we are wife, God is husband. With such metaphors, our identity is fashioned and completed by God.

If relationship implies connection and partnership, it also implies dynamism, growth, change, mutuality, demands, stumbles, disappointment, and forgiveness. It engages the heart as well as the mind. It leads us to experience both unbridled confidence, and desperate uncertainty.

One moment we might be saying: *"The Lord is my light and my salvation; whom shall I fear? The Lord is the stronghold of my life, of whom shall I be afraid?"* (Tehillim 27:1)

The next we might implore: *"My God, my God, why have you forsaken me? Why are the words of my cry far from my salvation? My God, I call by day but you do not answer; by night and there is no peace for me."* (Tehillim 22:3)

When God seems so very far away, the psalmist tries to erase the distance by reminding himself, and even more, reminding God, of the indelible nature of their connection:

> *You are the One who wrested me from my mother's womb; You gave me trust while I was yet upon my mother's breast. I have been cast upon You from my birth; You are my God from the moment of my birth.* (Tehillim 22:10-11)

You cannot turn away from me, God, the poet sings. Our history together is thick; you can no more disown me than I can disown you. Not because of laws, but because of what we have been through together. We are now part of one another.

Yehuda HaLevi also speaks of the dynamism of relationship, of turning away and turning back, of too much and too little, of taking the first step, and finding yourself already there.

"Lord, where shall I find you; high and hidden is your place; And where shall I not find you; the world is full of your glory.

I have sought your nearness, with all my heart I called you; and going out to meet you, I found you coming toward me."

Thinking of God as personality helps us feel that even as we seek God's presence, God seeks ours.

God as Lover

Shir HaShirim (the Song of Songs) was seen by the rabbis as the ultimate expression of a passionate and sometimes stormy relationship between the lovers God and the people Israel. They deeply desired one another. She says: *"By night on my bed I sought him whom my soul loves..."* He says: *"I come into my garden, my sister, my bride... Drink abundantly, my beloved."* And yet sometimes they hide and hurt each other. *"My beloved has turned*

Yehuda HaLevi (1075-1141) was one of the foremost Jewish poets and philosophers. He lived much of his life in Spain.

"But what is the nature of love that is due God? We should love God with a love so fervent and strong that our souls shall be bound up with love, and we should be constantly absorbed in this love, as it says 'And you shall love the Lord your God with all your heart and all your soul and all your might.'" (Rambam, Teshuvah 10:3)

12

away; and was gone... I sought him but could not find him, I called but he gave no answer."

The prophet Hosea speaks of God and Israel as more than lovers. He refers to Israel as God's wife, unfaithful though she be. His prophecy is full of the sounds of hurt and anger and sadness that comes with the loss of love and fidelity. But the hope that lies before us is that husband and wife will reconcile, and their relationship will turn into true partnership. *"And it shall be on that day,"* God says, *"that you shall call me Ishi [my husband] and not Baali [my master]."* And they will renew their vows saying, as we do every morning when we wrap the tefillin around our finger:

> *I will betroth you to me in righteousness and justice;*
> *I will betroth you to me in lovingkindness and compassion; I will betroth you to me in faithfulness, and you shall know the Lord.* (Hosea 3:21-22)

God as Beyond Knowability

Not everyone imagines God as personality, though.

Not everyone imagines that we can or even should speak of God in this way, for it is bound to lead us into trouble. Even the rabbis of old warned us against speaking of the realm of God: *"Whoever speculates on these four things, a pity on him: What is above; what is below; what is before; what is after."*

Maimonides begins his masterful code book, **Mishneh Torah**, with a statement of how we are to understand God if we are going to make sense of the world.

> "The basic principle of all principles and the pillar of all sciences is to realize that there is a First Being who brought every existing thing into being. All existing things, whether celestial, terrestrial, or belonging to an intermediate class exist only through His true Existence. If it could be supposed that He did not exist, it would follow that nothing else could possibly exist. If, however, it were supposed that all other things were non-existent, He alone would still exist. Their non-existence would not involve His non-existence. For all beings are in need of Him; but He, blessed be He, is not in need of them nor of any of them. This is what the prophet means when he says, "But the Eternal is the true God" (Jer. 10:10); that is, He alone is real, and nothing else has reality like His reality."

What is the difference between imagining Israel and God as lovers and imagining them as husband and wife? Why do you think both metaphors are used?

Moses Maimonides (1135-1204) is recognized as one of the most brilliant, original, and influential scholars of Jewish law and philosophy. He is also known as RaMBam, an acronym for Rabbi Moses ben Maimon. Among his other outstanding works is the **Mishneh Torah**, a massive, comprehensive legal code, arranged by topic.

13

This being is the God of the Universe, the Lord of all Earth. And He it is who controls the Sphere (of the Universe) with a power that is without end or limit, with a power that is without cessation. For the sphere is always revolving, and it is impossible for it to revolve without something making it revolve. God, blessed be He, it is, who, without hand or body, causes it to revolve. To acknowledge this is an affirmative precept, as it is said, "I am the Lord, thy God" (Ex. 20:2). And whoever permits the thought to enter his mind that there is another deity besides this God, violates a prohibition; as it is said, "Thou shalt have no other gods before me" (Ex. 20:3; Deut. 1:7), and denies the essence of religion--this doctrine being the great principle on which everything depends." (Fundamental Principles of the Torah, 2)[6]

The next grand principle we must understand - or try to understand - about God is this:

"God is One. He is not two nor more than two but One; so that none of the things existing in the universe to which the term "one" is applied is like unto His Unity; neither such a unit as a species which comprises many units, nor such a unit as a physical body which consists of parts and dimensions. His Unity is such that there is no other Unity like it in the world." (Book of Knowledge, 1:3)

To speak of God, which is the philosopher's way of knowing God, is to speak falsely. God is unique, indivisible, and complete. In short, God is one. But God's one is not our one; and God's unity is not our unity. To speak truly of God, we would have to create a whole new language, without any reference to human or physical characteristics. But of course we cannot. So, we speak about God in the only way we know how, choosing the imperfection of language over the isolation of silence. But we also must keep reminding ourselves that when we speak about God, we speak in the language of poetry. That is what Maimonides does.

Rabbi Haninah recognized the dilemma in the impulse toward speech and the insufficiency of speech. He tried to mediate it this way:

"A certain person, reciting prayers in the presence of Rabbi Haninah, said, "God the great, the valiant, the tremendous, the powerful, the strong, and the mighty." Rabbi Haninah said to him, "Have you now finished all the praises of the Master? Even the three terms: great, valiant and tremendous (hagadol, hagibur v'hanora) we should not have applied to God

Is Maimonides' explanation convincing? If so, then why do some people say that God doesn't exist? If not, why not?

Does believing Maimonides' concept necessarily reject belief in the modern scientific method?

How do you react to Maimonides' God? What is attractive about this vision of God? What is lacking? Why do you think Maimonides preferred this view of God?

What does Rabbi Haninah teach us about being over-zealous?

14

"As hard as we try - and try we must - there are no images through which to accurately describe God. 'Not knowing' what we mean when we say 'God' is not only acceptable, but ultimately the only true honest answer there is. The paradox is, in order to enter into a relationship with God, we must use human language, however imperfect, to describe that relationship."
- S.L.

had Moses not mentioned them in the law, and had not men of the great Synagogue come forward and established their use in the prayer service. And you say all this!" (Berakhot 33b)

The insufficiency of speech and the impulse to speak are best displayed in this hasidic tale:

"The rav once asked a disciple who had just entered the room: Moshe what do we mean when we say God? The disciple was silent. The rav asked him again, and yet a third time, and still the disciple was silent.

Finally, the rav asked, Why are you silent?

The disciple responded, because I do not know.

Do you think I know, said the rav. But I must say it, for it is so, and therefore, I must say it: God is definitely there, and except for God nothing is definitely there, and this is God.[7]

Perhaps that is all that the believer can say.

The Ein Sof and...

One remarkable effort to merge the unspeakable and the speakable is found in the theology of kabbalah. While there are many strands of kabbalistic thought, each differing somewhat from the others, the most systematic, influential and enduring kabbalistic view of God is the one articulated by **Isaac Luria**.

Isaac Luria was known as the Ari, the Holy Lion. Luria, a student of kabbalah all his life, spent his last years in Safed, the center of kabbalistic study. He died at the age of 38, in the year 1572.

This system is described for the popular audience in a book entitled God and the Big Bang by Rabbi Daniel Matt.

Before Creation, there was only *Ein Sof*, God as infinity (the ineffable God, the God about whom we cannot speak). But if *Ein Sof* pervaded all space, how could there be room for anything other than God? How could the process of divine emanation begin? Pondering such questions in the Galilean city of Safed in the sixteenth century, the kabbalist Isaac Luria concluded that the first act of creation was not emanation, but withdrawal: "Before the creation of the universe, *Ein Sof* withdrew Itself into Its essence, from Itself to Itself within Itself. Within Its essence,

It left an empty space, in which It could emanate and create...When *Ein Sof* withdrew Its presence all around in every direction, It left a vacuum in the middle, surrounded on all sides by the light of *Ein Sof*, empty precisely in the middle.

This is *tsimtsum*, literally "contraction," but here implying the withdrawal by which God made room for something other than God. The primordial vacuum carved out by *tsimtsum* was a pregnant void, the site of creation: no more than an infinitesimal point in relation to *Ein Sof*, yet spacious enough to house the cosmos. But the vacuum was not really empty. It retained a trace, a residue of the light of *Ein Sof*.

As *Ein Sof* began to unfold, a ray of light was channeled into the vacuum through vessels. Everything went smoothly at first, but some less capacious, less translucent vessels could not withstand the power of the light and shattered. Most of the light returned to its infinite source, "to the mother's womb." But the rest, falling as sparks along with shards of the shattered vessels, was eventually trapped in material existence. Our task is to liberate these sparks and restore them to divinity... By living ethically and spiritually, we raise the sparks and thereby bring about *tikkun:* the "repair" or mending of the cosmos.[8]

The Ein Sof is beyond language and beyond thought. To live only with the belief in God who is Ein Sof is to live in spiritual isolation.

...Shekhinah

So the kabbalists created a mediating structure, composed of The **Ten Sefirot**, that represent the flow of the stream of life, traveling from the Ein Sof to the Shekhinah, the manifestation of God found in the material world. More than just a mediator, this model enables us to endow our every act with cosmic import.

The Shekhinah is in exile from the Ein Sof, even as the Jews were in exile from their homeland and are in exile from a world of peace, a world repaired. Every mitzvah done with the right intent can repair a piece of the broken world. Not only can God's deeds comfort us. According to the kabbalists, our deeds can comfort God.

The kabbalists were responsible for returning this idea of the Shekhinah to the common Jew. In early rabbinic thought, the Shekhinah was the name given to God's presence among us. It is the feeling of God's comfort when we are lonely or in pain;

"God is everything that exists, though everything that exists is not God. It is present in everything, and everything comes into being from it. Nothing is devoid of its divinity. Everything is within it. It is within everything and outside of everything. There is nothing but it." - S.L.

While Ein Sof is indescribable, the mystics do describe the **Ten Sefirot**: "the various stages of God's inner life and the dynamics of divine personality." They are listed from highest to lowest:

1. **Keter (Crown)** - Undifferentiated oneness, roughly the same as infinity.
2. **Chokhmah (Wisdom)**
3. **Binah (Understanding)**
4. **Chesed (Love)**
5. **Din (Judgment)** - also called Gevurah (Power)
6. **Tiferet (Beauty)** - also called Rachamim (Compassion)
7. **Netzach (Eternity)**
8. **Hod (Splendor)**
9. **Yesod (Foundation)** - the light and power of the preceding sefirot are channeled through yesod to the tenth sefirah.
10. **Malkhut (Kingdom)** or **Shekhinah (God's Presence)**

16

God's joy when we are happy; God's companionship and support when we turn our lives to acts of holiness. What are such acts? Mishnah 3:7 in Pirkei Avot tells us when the Shekhinah joins us:

> Rabbi Halafta, of Kefar Hananiah, taught:
>
> When ten persons sit together and study Torah, the Shekhinah hovers over them, as it is written, *"God is present in the divine assembly"* (Tehillim 82:1).
>
> Where do we learn that this applies also to five? From the verse *"He has established His band on earth"* (Amos 9:6).
>
> Where do we learn that this applies also to three? From the verse *"He judges in the midst of the judges"* (Tehillim 82:1).
>
> Where do we learn that this applies also to two? From the verse *"Then those who fear the Lord conversed with one another and the Lord listened and heard"* (Malachi 3:16).
>
> From where do we learn that this is true even of one? From the verse *"In every place where I cause My Name to be mentioned, I will come to you and bless you"* (Shemot 20:21).

If God is everywhere, why do we feel sometimes that God is so far away? The hasidim ask and answer the very same question this way: "Where do you find God?" they ask. "Wherever you let God in." God may be all around us, but God is only in our hearts if we let God in.

God as the Fullness of Life - Kaplan

A thoroughly twentieth-century view of God was articulated by the founder of the Reconstructionist movement, Rabbi Mordecai Kaplan, who for many years taught at the Jewish Theological Seminary. Kaplan writes in his grand work: The Meaning Of God....

> The human mind cannot rest until it finds order in the universe. It is this form-giving trait that is responsible for modern scientific theory. That same need is also operative in formulating a view of the cosmos... But there is one underlying assumption in all these efforts at giving a consistent meaning to life... that the world of nature is a cosmos, not a chaos... that science cannot dispense with what Einstein has appropriately named "cosmic religion," the faith that nature is meaningful and hence divine.[9]

What are the benefits of a theology which includes the concepts of both Ein Sof and Shekhinah?

"Kaplan's theology is significant in that it requires human action and human involvement. God needs us. It is our actions that bring the force of moral good to the world." - D.C.

17

Human nature leads us to the divine just as much as it leads us to eat, think, create, desire and progress. The act of seeking meaning - one of humanity's most significant impulses - is an act of faith.

For Kaplan, God is not a supernatural Creator who is independent of, and apart from, the world. Rather:

> It is only as the sum of everything in the world that renders life significant and worthwhile - or holy - that God can be worshipped by man. Godhood can have no meaning for us apart from human ideals of truth, goodness and beauty, interwoven in a pattern of holiness. To believe in God is to reckon with life's creative forces, tendencies and potentialities as forming an organic unity and as giving meaning to life by virtue of that unity. Life has meaning for us when it elicits from us the best of which we are capable, and fortifies us against the worst that may befall us... Thus in the very process of human self-fulfillment, in the very striving after the achievement of salvation, we identify ourselves with God, and God functions in us.[10]

As all good theologies, this one too lays certain claims on its adherents. It answers the question, "Now that I know that I believe like this, what am I to do?"

> We must accustom ourselves to find God in the complexities of our experience and behavior. *"Seek ye me and live"* (Amos 5:4) To seek God, to inquire after Him, to try to discern his reality is religion in action. The ardent and strenuous search for God in all that we know and feel and do is the true equivalent of *"Thou shalt love the Lord thy God with all thy heart, with all thy soul and with all thy might."* Only by way of participation in human affairs and strivings are we to seek God."[11]

For Kaplan, we become most godly when we act most human. ☞27

God as the One Who Inspires Response - Heschel

Abraham Joshua Heschel follows a different path toward God. He is not so interested in describing the way we understand God as in describing the way we respond to God.

> "The theme of theology is the content of believing. The theme of the present study is the act of believing."[12]

Kaplan defines "holy" as "significant and worthwhile." How would you define the word "holy?"

What is it that you believe Kaplan is asking you to do?

"God is to be found in each act that we choose to do or choose not to do. The search for God is a daily endeavor informed by our own choices, not a passive experience where we wait for God to come knocking, or even simply an awareness of God's presence." - D.C.

18

For Heschel, just as God's goodness is to be found in the detail of doing, so is the fullness of human life. Heschel imagined each of us as an artist, our lives as our masterpieces, and each act as adding color, boldness and definition to our work.

Heschel uses "man" in the generic sense of humanity.

For Heschel, believing is grounded in relationship, in the way two partners act in the presence of each other. It is in that very notion of relationship, in the awareness that humanity can seek God, that the magic happens.

> "The grand premise of religion is that man is able to surpass himself; that man who is part of this world may enter into a relationship with Him who is greater than the world."

Heschel sees God all around him.

> "The Maimonidean creed is based upon the premise that it is in ideas that ultimate reality comes to expression. To the Biblical man [and to Heschel himself], however, it is in events, not only in ideas that ultimate reality comes to expression... To the Jewish mind, the understanding of God is not achieved by referring in a Greek way to timeless qualities of a Supreme Being, to ideas of goodness or perfection, but rather by sensing the living acts of His concern, to His dynamic attentiveness to man. We speak not of His goodness in general but of His compassion for the individual man in a particular situation. God's goodness is not a cosmic force but a specific act of compassion. We do not know it as it is but as it happens."[13]

Yes there is a transcendent God for Heschel, but it is the imminent, palpable presence of God in our lives that matters. And for Heschel, that Divine presence is not hidden. It can be seen in the face of each and every person on earth, for we are all made in the image of God. ☞<u>28</u>

God as Playwright

Rabbi Yochanan Muffs is a Bible scholar who teaches at the Jewish Theological Seminary in New York. In an extraordinary book, called <u>Love and Joy</u>, Muffs has a chapter which explores the nature of the role of the prophets. In this chapter, Muffs imagines God as a cosmic playwright, Torah as the play, the world as the stage, and the Jewish people as the actors. And if we bracket the role set aside for the prophets, who are no more, we have a most suggestive image of God and us.

To call Torah the play does not sufficiently capture its power or nature warns Rabbi Muffs. Rather, we should imagine that first there was pure play, the play as it was in the mind of God. But that was not enough.

God wanted to see the play. "To bring this play to fruition was an unbearable urge." For the play to move from the mind of God to the stage, it had to be translated into the language of earth and humanity. God built the stage and the props and the lighting, and gave the script over to the actors God had chosen.

Now this play was not written word for word; rather it was more like a "treatment," an outline. It was up to the actors, through their collective wisdom, insight and experience, to fill out and fill in the details of the play.

God promised to always be in the wings "and if they departed too radically from the script, [God] would set them on the right path by means of hints delivered by his agents [the prophets]. The play has begun, the actors have appeared, and the dramatist still haunts the wings of the theatre, desperately worried about the fate of the play."[14]

As actors, we are more than partners in God's creation. We are the ones who make the play real, who carry it forward. The play can only live through us; not any one of us alone, but all of us together. Knowing we are actors on a stage raises our awareness that every deed we perform, every word we utter, is watched and fretted over by God. The pressure is intense but the reward is great, for we are the center of God's attention, and the ones who carry forward God's dream.

Change and Responsiveness

Our personal beliefs and approaches to God grow and change as we grow and change. They are crafted from a combination of up-bringing, education, personal experiences, personal predilections adventurousness and more. All human relationships are dynamic. Should our relationship with or toward God be any different?

But if our belief and responses to God change over time, does that mean that God is nothing more than an image of our own making? Or does that mean - absurd as it is - that the nature of God changes according to our whims? or that our beliefs today are false because they are likely to change tomorrow?

An image the kabbalists employ can help us understand the apparently changeable yet stable nature of God. Imagine that the **divine emanations** are water, clear, pure and all part of one body. Yet when the emanations meet the physical world (and the limitations of our mind), they are forced into vessels, each one a different color. As they flow through these vessels, these

Is it reassuring, exciting or frightening to think we are the actors of God's play? How would such a belief affect what you do tomorrow?

The **divine emanations** can be thought of as rays of holiness that flow from God toward the world.

20

"One can think of God as the entire spectrum of color, all the colors in the world. God is white light, bright and illuminating our world. But the light is far too bright for us to look at directly, so we hold it up to the prism of our own needs. We see the blue of support when we are tired, the yellow of love when we are engaged in a holy activity, etc. God is truly all things, but we can perceive only one element of God at a time because God is simply too huge for us humans to comprehend." - D.C.

Aquilla was a Roman aristocrat who converted first to Christianity and then to Judaism. He later translated the Hebrew Bible into Greek under the supervision of the leading scholars in the period after the destruction of the second Temple.

emanations appear to us to be blue, green, orange, red. Or, in the language of theology, they appear as God's love, judgment, anger, compassion, commandment, and so on. But in truth, these apparent changes reside only in the interaction between the emanations and us, not in the nature of the emanation itself.

Our teachers throughout the ages were very aware of the difficulties of imagining a relationship between God and humanity: the Perfect in relationship with the imperfect; the Indescribable being described; the Infinite beheld by the finite.

They were sensitive to the necessary awkwardness of God being seen as personality, and as needing us even as we need God. And yet, they also understood the necessity of holding onto such a conundrum if the covenant between Jews and God was to endure. Rabbi Shimon bar Yohai was perhaps brashest when he interpreted the verse in Isaiah (43:10): "*You are my witnesses and I am God*," as follows: "when you are My witnesses, I am God. When you are not my witnesses, I am not, as it were, God."

It may be brash but it is not blasphemy to imagine that our changing awareness and temperament affects God and God's response to us. Time and again, Jewish tradition reassures us that seeing ourselves as true covenantal partners, that is, as partners who make a claim on God, is appropriate. A midrash helps us come to terms with this paradox: *"When Abram was ninety years old and nine, the Lord appeared to him and said: "I am El Shaddai, walk with me and be wholehearted"* (Bereshit 17:1).

The name of God here, *El Shaddai,* is midrashically interpreted as meaning "God, who is enough." In fact, God is too much for us. Yet, in God's desire to be with us, in God's desire to enable us to be with God, God responds to us according to our needs, according to our abilities. **Aquilla** in fact translated this verse as: "I am faithful to each person, according to his deeds." Since our needs, desires, abilities, and tendencies change and grow throughout our lives, so will our images and attachment to God.

So may it always be.

EXERCISE 1: Faith Interview:[15]

A problem many people face is a kind of loneliness in regard to their feelings and questions regarding faith and God. Too often we believe that because we have questions, we are, therefore, non-believers and write ourselves out of our religious tradition. Nothing could be further from the truth. Religious people of all times have had deep and fundamental questions. That's what being religiously alive is all about. The problem today is that we don't share our questions and doubts with each other. Be as honest as possible in answering the following questions. If you do this exercise with another person, after one person has been the "interviewer," switch roles.

1. If there is a God, how do you picture God?

2. Do you talk to God yourself?

3. Have you ever felt God talking to you, or have you ever felt God's presence?

4. What are some of your doubts about God?

5. If God is good, how can God permit evil in the world?

6. Do you know of any differences between the Jewish conceptions of God and Christian conceptions of God?

7. Is there anything that makes you angry about God?

8. Has God ever answered any of your prayers?

9. Does God still function in the world as described in the Bible?

10. What is a miracle? Do you believe in miracles?

11. Do you believe in life after death? What form does it take?

12. Do you believe God punishes the sinners and rewards the righteous?

13. Do you think that the Jewish people has been chosen by God for something special?

14. If you were God, what would you do differently?

15. Do you pray to God more when you are sick and in trouble? Do you think more about God when someone you love is in trouble or in danger?

16. Do you thank God for the good things in your life as well as relating God to the bad things that happen?

22

EXERCISE 2: Godbeliefs[16]

Adapted from Howard Wasserman, Ellen Z. Charry, Diane King, Jerome Ruderman, eds., Idea Cookbook (Philadelphia: Board of Jewish Education, United Synagogue of America, 1976).

		Yes	No	Not Sure
1.	I believe that God created the world and directs the happenings in it.	___	___	___
2.	I believe that God does not interfere in the affairs of people.	___	___	___
3.	I believe that the world came into being by accident.	___	___	___
4.	I believe that God is aware of what I do.	___	___	___
5.	I believe that God can answer prayer.	___	___	___
6.	I believe that God punishes evil.	___	___	___
7.	I believe that God intended us never to understand certain things about the world.	___	___	___
8.	I believe that my concepts about God differ from the Torah's concept of God.	___	___	___
9.	I believe that even if there were no people, God would still exist.	___	___	___
10.	I believe that God decided what is good and what is evil.	___	___	___
11.	I believe that God gets involved in human affairs when God wants to.	___	___	___
12.	I believe that God rewards good.	___	___	___
13.	I believe that God exists independently of, and outside of people.	___	___	___
14.	I believe that prayer is an attempt to talk to God.	___	___	___
15.	I believe that the Torah is the word of God.	___	___	___
16.	I believe that God listens to prayer.	___	___	___
17.	I believe that "God" is a term that people use to describe their best hopes for humanity.	___	___	___
18.	I believe God exists only Inside of people.	___	___	___
19.	I believe that praying can benefit the person who prays, even if God doesn't listen.	___	___	___
20.	I believe that "God" is an idea people use to describe those things beyond human understanding	___	___	___
21.	I believe prayer can have an effect on people's lives regardless of what they think about God.	___	___	___

What else do you believe about God?

EXERCISE 3: The Names of God[17]

Below is a long list of names, appellations, and descriptions of God found in our tradition. They are gathered from the Siddur, other Jewish literature, and the writings of modern theologians. This list is not complete. Other translations could have been used for many of the names. Find a quiet place and mark those names which match your beliefs or feel right to you. Your list need not be long--just sincere. If you wish, share your preferences with others in the group. What other names would you like to add?

1. Adonai, "My Lord"

2. Father

3. Mother

4. The True God

5. The Divinity

6. The Fear of Isaac

7. Mighty One of Jacob

8. El, The God of (The Patriarch) Israel

9. Most High

10. Everlasting God

11. God Almighty

12. God of Vision

13. God of the Covenant

14. Husband

15. Everlasting Rock

16. Ancient God

17. Everlasting Arms

18. Everlasting Life

19. YHWH, "The One Who Causes to Be"

20. I am that I am

21. Lord of Hosts

22. Creator of Heaven and Earth

23. Holy One

24. Holy One of Israel

25. Shepherd of Israel

26. The Place

27. King of Israel

28. The God of Truth

29. Artist

30. Praiseworthy God

31. Guardian of Israel

32. Shield of Abraham

33. Rock of Israel

34. King over the king of kings

35. The Name

36. The Holy One, Praised be He

37. Heaven

38. Peace

39. Lover

40. Judge of the Earth

41. The Awesome One

42. My Rock

43. Eternal One of Israel

44. Shekhinah

45. Lover of His People Israel

46. The Ransomer

47. The Redeemer

48. The Guide

49. God of Abraham, Isaac and Jacob, Sarah, Rebecca, Rachel and Leah

50. The One Who Listens to My Prayer

51. The Mighty One

24

52. The Heroic One

53. Rescuer

54. Reviver of the Dead

55. Father of Mercy

56. The Merciful One

57. The Might

58. The Faithful One

59. Lord of the Universe

60. Ein Sof

61. The Infinite

62. King of Compassion and Mercy

63. The Good One

64. He Who Is Merciful

65. Maker of Peace

66. "Thankworthy" God

67. The Holy King

68. Master of All

69. The Creator

70. Our Shepherd

71. Our Healer

72. The Living God of Majesty

73. Sovereign

74. The Compassionate One

75. The Patient One

76. The Bountiful One

77. The One Who is Forgiveness

78. The Generous One

79. Hidden of Hiddens

80. Ancient of Ancients

81. The First Cause

82. World-Soul

83. Absolute Spirit

84. Absolute Rest

85. The Power That Makes for Salvation

86. The Power That Makes for The Fulfillment of All Valid Ideals

After reading this list it should become obvious that in our tradition there are many images of God. No one need accept all of them. This allows, or encourages, a flexibility of belief which stems from the notion that in Judaism (1) what one does in life is often more important than what one believes. We show our love and belief in God through our love and actions on behalf of humanity; and (2) that many different approaches to God can all be true.

Based on Robert Blinder, "What's in a Name?" Genesis -- A Synagogue of Our Times, St. Louis. Missouri.

EXERCISE 4: Awesomeness of the Earth

Imagine that you are in the Space Shuttle looking down at the awesome sight of the planet Earth. What are some of the emotions you might experience? What are some of the questions you might ponder? Now read again the words of Barukh She'amar. How do you get to know God through this scene?

_____

_____

_____

_____

_____

_____

EXERCISE 5: Images of the Law

A central image of Jewish lore is Moses, an old but strong man, descending from Mount Sinai, carrying the tablets of the Ten Commandments carved by God in his arms. This image captures a core Jewish theological belief - that God's greatest gift to the Jewish people is the law and it is through giving this law that God expresses's God's love.

Yet, the Jewish people have a gift to offer in return. Through obeying the law, we express our love for God. What image might capture the Jewish people's acceptance of the law? Explain how this image might do so.

_____

_____

_____

_____

_____

_____

EXERCISE 6: Attributes of a Judge

List and describe some of the attributes and qualifications of a judge.

_____

_____

_____

_____

_____

_____

EXERCISE 7: The People's Court

You are the defending attorney. How do you defend humanity in front of the supreme judge? List the arguments you would use.

_____

_____

_____

_____

_____

_____

EXERCISE 8: The Nature of Relationships

What are your relationships like with different people - parents, grandparents, boy/girlfriends, best friends, etc? How is each relationship similar and how does each differ? Compare how your relationship with God is similar and/or different.

_____

_____

_____

_____

_____

_____

EXERCISE 9: The Quality of Godhood

According to Kaplan, what might it mean to "follow" God, or rather "to possess the quality of Godhood?" Can you identify some moments or deeds in your life that you believe possess "the quality of Godhood?"

_____

_____

_____

_____

_____

_____

EXERCISE 10: Human Relationship with God

When Heschel marched for civil rights with Martin Luther King, Jr. from Selma to Montgomery, he said: "I felt my legs were praying."

For Heschel, the march was an event through which we could make God's presence known in the world and through which we could reach toward God. Can you think of other acts or events through which human beings can reach toward God?

_____

_____

_____

_____

_____

_____

Chapter 2:
Definitions of Spirituality

"Be holy for I the Lord your God am holy" (Vayikra 19:2)

Our understanding of God begins not with answers, but with questions. Many questions. Where does life come from? Why was I born? How do we know right from wrong? Does anything really matter? How can I live a life of meaning?

For many of us, the twentieth century was a time when we almost lost hope even in asking those questions. And as the questions faded, so did God's presence.

The modern quest for spirituality, then, is an effort to recapture the questions. It is a renewal of the search for meaning, the quest for purpose, the journey toward the divine that propels the human enterprise on earth. It is a renewal of that sense of wonder that the age of industry and technology almost snuffed out.

Reason, which once threatened to take us away from God, is now bringing us back to God. As creatures of reason, we seek to discover sense and order and purpose in the universe. Living without order and purpose is like dancing without music. Spirituality is the music of our lives. And God is the conductor. Today, more and more people are seeking the score and playing it in their daily lives.

This is very good. And yet, we must be careful. Sometimes we get tripped up by the score, or hit a false note. Sometimes, we confuse a chord with a melody, the part with the whole, the helpful with the holy. Technology, nationalism, science, medicine, humanism, progress, and affluence have all vied for the role of God. This is modern idolatry. Yet, none of these can become our covenantal partner, none can offer comfort, or salvation; none can answer our fundamental questions of purpose, reason, morals, ethics, values, right and wrong.

On Believers and Skeptics

As we live our lives, we continually seek the source that remains when all else fades, the source from which all else flows, the source that serves as our eternal refuge. As we grow older, we seek even more: our place within this source. Some of us - either readily or

Heschel once said that if there is no question, there can be no answer. What do you think he meant by that? What is the difference between a statement and an answer? Why should we care so much about questions?

30

after much hard work - are able to say, we have found that source, and we call the source God, Adonai, El Shaddai, Ribono shel Olam, Tzuri v'goali. We can feel God's presence in everything we do, in every breath we take. *"And God breathed the breath of life into the human."* (Bereshit 2:7) As it was at creation of Adam, so it is with us.

Others of us feel a bit lost, uncertain, or uncomfortable with the vocabulary of spirituality, unsure of the quest. But we too are eager to believe; we want to know if there is more to life than material existence. So we keep our eyes and ears and most of all, our hearts open.

Still others of us are a bit skeptical. Perhaps we feel an emptiness where fullness should be; perhaps we feel abandoned or mistreated; perhaps we feel that there is no God at all.

Truth be told, throughout our lives, many of us find ourselves flowing in and out of these different attitudes, now a seeker, now a doubter, hopefully, eventually a believer. It is very rare to hold onto a static belief in God; or a frozen sense of one's place in the cosmos.☞39

Since belief - or the lack of belief - changes over a lifetime, the spiritual quest is never complete. It needs to be constantly pursued, renewed and replenished, both for believers and skeptics.

If we call **spirituality** the quest for ultimate answers, then the question for each of us is not: yes spirituality or no spirituality, but which spirituality? What kind of spiritual quest will we pursue? What language will we use?

Weaving One's Quest

Lives don't just happen; they are woven by their owners out of the acts of our daily lives on a loom shaped by a guiding ideology or belief. Everything we do adds a weave, a color, and dimension to the design of our lives.

What guides the design; what inspires our choices, our movements? In Judaism the answer is: Torah. Torah helps us answer the fundamental questions of our lives: Is life meaningful or empty; can I bring goodness to the world or am I powerless; can I offer love; can I learn to comfort; can I dare to hope; can I bear to wait? When I stumble, what will help me up? When things are bleak, from where can I draw new strength? All these are questions of the spirit. And all these are addressed by the spiritual Jewish works we call Torah.

What do we gain by believing in God?

Spirituality is a question, more than an answer; a seeking, more than a finding. As such, it includes us all.

"I lift my eyes to the mountain, from where will my help come?" asks the psalmist. How would you answer?

"My help comes from God," the psalmist responds, *"Creator of heaven and earth."* (Tehillim 121:1-2) The psalmist is in need, and pulls himself out of despair by declaring his trust in God.

The psalms are the records of individual spiritual quests; records of someone's weaving together hope, wonderment, rejoicing, despair, and confidence. We can learn from these psalmists and be enriched by them. Yet, no one spiritual quest is like any other. Each quest is borne by the web of an individual's own upbringing, training, experiences, community, appetites, and inclinations. Even in Judaism there are different ways to speak the language of spirituality.

Rabbi Neil Gillman teaches that Judaism provides three models of spirituality, "three answers to the question: What does God demand of me above all?" The three models he labels: the behavioral ("God demands that we do certain things"); the intellectual ("God demands study"); and the pietistic ("God demands passion").[1]

At times, these three models might be in tension, as seen in the struggles between the early hasidim (who emphasized piety and passion) and the mitnagdim (who emphasized punctilious behavior). But they are never separated. All three are needed. And all three are grounded in Torah.

Mitzvah, Study and Prayer

For Judaism, spirituality resides in action. It is a way of doing, a way of responding, and not just a way of thinking or being.

"Blessed are you, Ruler of the Universe, who sanctified us by your commandments, commanding us to..." - do something. Study Torah, put on tefillin, light Shabbat candles.

We are sanctified, that is, made holy, by doing God's bidding, by following the time-honored traditions of our ancestors, by helping one another, and by responding with acts which are the brushstrokes of our lives.

Rabbi Arthur Green, in the introduction to his two volume anthology entitled <u>Jewish Spirituality</u>, frames the topic as follows:

Literally, Torah is the first part of the Hebrew Bible and refers to the Five Books of Moses. Yet over the years, every work that was inspired by the Torah, that is, all midrash, halakhah, mishnah, gemara, literature and philosophy, is also called Torah. It is that meaning that is employed here.

Of the three models of spirituality taught by Rabbi Gillman, which do you feel best expresses your own Jewishness?

Life in the presence of God - the cultivation of a life in the ordinary world bearing the holiness once associated with sacred space and time, with Temple and with holy days - is perhaps as close as one can come to a definition of "spirituality" that is native to the Jewish tradition....[2]

Spirituality can be, is meant to be, *lived,* not just on special occasions but in the *everyday.* Spirituality can be, is meant to be, found in the ways we work, play, speak, learn, and love. As the Torah says:

> *For this commandment which I command you this day is not too wondrous for you, nor is it far off. It is not in heaven that you should say, 'who will go up for us to heaven and bring it to us and cause us to hear it so we may do it.' It is not from across the sea, that you should say, 'Who will cross the sea and bring it back to us and cause us to hear it so we may do it.' Rather it is very close to you, in your mouths and in your hearts, that you may do it.* (Devarim 30:11-14)

Jewish spirituality lies within our reach, literally within our hands and at our fingertips, in the tasks we do and the relationships we enter, everyday. It can be sought through our sacred rituals and through our personal interactions. It can be sought through the language that we use, in the favors we perform and the slights we choose to overlook. *"It has been told to you what is good and what God requires of you: only to do justice, love kindness and walk humbly with your God."* (Michah 6:8) This, too, is everyday spirituality.☞40

The Gift of Awareness

There is no accidental spirituality. Spirituality requires awareness, which leads to higher moments of awareness.

Rabbi Rachel Cowan describes her experiences of awareness this way: "On rare occasions, I experienced the overpowering sense that my small inner self had burst through a crevice into the eternal."[3]

The Torah crafts the language of Jewish spirituality as the search for holiness: *"Be holy for I the Lord your God am holy"* (Vayikra 19:2). Holiness is not accidental. It demands attention, intention and response. It is grounded in our awareness of our covenant with God, and our likeness to God. This awareness of the ability to be holy

"The critical element of spirituality may be humility. We sense that there is something beyond where we are and we must recognize that in order to find that Something, we must acknowledge that our strength is not enough. It is only when we acknowledge that there is something beyond our grasp that we find that Something coming forward to meet us." - D.C.

33

opens the way for us to seek our place with God, and to find meaning and purpose in our lives.

Holiness is like love. It is an attitude that infuses and inspires everything we do. With or without holiness, we may look the same to the world. But the world looks different to us.

It is through being aware of this call to holiness, grounded in the source of the Holy, that Judaism helps us build a life of meaning.

> Then I heard the voice of my Lord saying, "Whom will I send? Who will go for us?" and I responded, "Hineni, here I am, send me." (Isaiah 6:8)

Just as in Isaiah, so too with us: God calls. It is up to us to answer. Spirituality cannot be imposed. *"All is in the hands of heaven except the fear of heaven."* (Berakhot 33b) God can only find a home in a willing heart.

"The Kotzker rebbe asked: "Where is the dwelling place of God?"

His visitors laughed and said, "What a thing to ask. Is not the whole world full of God's glory?"

The Kotzker replied: "God dwells wherever you let God in."

Even for those of us who cannot believe, the tradition has an answer. "So what if you do not believe in God?" we are asked. "God believes in you."

Spirituality Through Community

Turning ourselves toward God is the beginning, not the end, of the spiritual quest. Once we open ourselves to God, once we say "hineni," we open ourselves anew to the world around us.

"The Kotzker Rebbe had a rather sober view of reality. He was visited one day by Reb Yaakov Aryeh of Radzimon. Now, the Kotzker was not given to small talk. So after a moment or two, he turned to Reb Yaakov and asked: "Why was humankind created? Why are we humans here on this earth?"

And Reb Yaakov said, "Each person is created in order to work on their soul, to repair their soul."

Do you agree that holiness is like love? What does it mean that with holiness, "the world looks different to us?"

34

The Kotzker didn't like that answer at all. So he thundered at Reb Yaakov, "That's idolatry, that's self worship; that's not why God put us on this earth. We were created to keep the heavens aloft. Without us, the heavens would collapse."[4]

We were not put on this earth solely to find ourselves, or fulfill ourselves, or to pursue our private, interior spiritual quests. We are not granted the insights of holiness solely for personal enlightenment. We are granted the insights of holiness to connect us with others and to help improve the world.

The world is one interlocking unit. The earth supports us and we must support the earth; God supports us and we must support God; our loved ones support us and we must support them. To turn inward is to shift our portion of the weight to others and to risk collapse. Spirituality in Judaism is not solely, or even primarily, a personal affair. It is significantly a communal enterprise with cosmic implications.

> *And God spoke to Moses saying: Speak to the <u>entire</u> <u>assembly</u> of the <u>family</u> of Israel, and say to them: "You shall be holy, for I the Lord your God am holy."*
> (Vayikra 19:1-2)

Why this strange formulation, the commentators wonder. Why this triple emphasis on the *kahal*, the community: "entire," "assembly," and "family of Israel?"

The Sefat Emet explains: "Holiness can be attained only within *klal yisrael,* as it says, *"all the assembly, all of them, are holy; and God is in their midst."* (Bamidbar 16:3) We cannot bear the weight or brilliance of holiness alone. We need each other, all of us. I am only holy when I am joined with all of you.

"Israel is not a people of definers of religion but *a people of witnesses* to God's concern for humanity."[5]

It is when we act as a people, and define ourselves as part of a people, that we can act as witnesses for God.☞40

Remembering God, Remembering Self

What do you think it means to be witnesses for God's concern? For me, it means that we are to reflect God's presence to one

What are our responsibilities to the community? What, in turn, does the community give us?

Does community help us in finding meaning within ritual observance? Does it help us to better understand Judaism?

35

another; to radiate God's light for one another; to see the face of God in one another; and to perform those tasks that mirror God's compassion. Why are we commanded not to make an image of God? asks Heschel. Not because it blasphemes God, but because it blasphemes us. For we are made in the image of God. To make an idol is to counterfeit humanity, to deny our role as partners with God, and to create false witnesses.

To be witnesses of God's concern for humanity is a full-time job, carried on through the work of our everyday. It requires constant awareness of our presence before God and God's presence before us. The Hasidim call this constant awareness *devekut,* cleaving.

"*Devekut* means to remember God and your love for Him always and at all times, so that you never remove your mind from Him, when you are walking on the way or lying down or rising up."

The image that tradition offers to connote this notion of full, constant and dedicated awareness of God is called *maaseh merkavah*, the journeys of the divine chariot. Rabbi Yitzhak Buxbaum in his recent book, <u>Jewish Spiritual Practices</u>, defines it this way:

> The idea is that a chariot is directed in all its movements by the charioteer who comes within it, and whose hands are on the reins. [If you are the chariot and God is the charioteer, then], all your actions, speech and thoughts will be directed by God, who is within you.[6]

We do not become God's puppets. That could never be, for free will is part of the essence of humanity, part of the nature of being made in God's image. God has no need of us if we have no free will. The image rather conveys the notion that every action becomes an intimate response to our awareness of God's presence within us, and every task we perform is done in response to our understanding of God's will.

Facing God-Ward

In short, to be a witness is to turn ourselves to God. The word most commonly used to describe this attitude of spirituality is *kavvanah.* It is translated as concentration, orientation, focus, meditation, attentiveness, or directedness. *Kavvanah* comes from the Hebrew root meaning to face in the direction of. Perhaps then the best translation might be facing God-ward.

What is the task of a good witness? How does Heschel's understanding of witness differ from the definition of a trial witness? How can one serve as God's witness everyday?

"Another way of viewing the chariot metaphor is by viewing ourselves as being the horse, and the chariot as the effect of our choices. God directs us, but we know that we can give a horse directions and the horse may choose to turn a different way, or bolt and run. Although we have trained the horse, the horse retains free will. So too, the individual, driven by the Holy Charioteer, directed by God, is free to make his/her own choices." - D.C.

36

It is appropriate to recite a kavvanah for almost anything we want to do well.

Rabbi Nehunia ben Kana would say a kavvanah before he went in to teach:

"May it be your will, Adonai, my God, that no misunderstandings or confusion arise because of my teachings, and may my colleagues and students value my learning and may I value theirs."

Upon leaving the beit midrash, he would say:

"I thank you God that you placed my portion in life among the students of Torah" (Berakhot 28b).

Rav would ask God to protect him from speaking lies; excite him about a life of mitzvot, and save him from those who wished him harm.

How can we help ourselves remember "that question?"

Imagine something you will be doing this coming week for which you would want to write a kavvanah. Take a moment and compose your own kavannah. Then, on that day, before you begin the deed, take out the kavvanah and read it, aloud. It may just change the way you do it.

With all that we do, it is easy to become distracted, to lose our God-compass, to become disoriented, to fill with the mundane the space that should be filled by God. Even the most pious among us are subject to the temptations and distractions of the every day. What we all need is some device that continually orients us in the God-ward direction, just as the *mizrah* in traditional homes points us in the direction of Jerusalem. Blessings said before certain tasks remind us of who we are; wearing a kippah or a mezuzah reminds us of Whose we are. Some Jews recite a kavvanah before reciting the appropriate blessing before performing a mitzvah: "Here I am, prepared and attentive, ready to perform the mitzvah of my Creator...." This kavvanah is a little tug, a reminder, a re-orientation, helping the speakers to set their sights through the task at hand to the God who lies beyond the mitzvah.

"In Ropchitz, the town where Rabbi Naftali lived, it was the custom for the rich people whose houses stood at the far end of town to hire men to watch over their property at night. Late one evening, when Rabbi Naftali was skirting the woods which circled the city, he met such a watchman walking up and down.

"For whom do you work," he asked the watchman, and the man told him.

Then the man inquired in turn, "And for whom do you work?"

The words struck the rabbi like a shaft. "I am not working for anyone just yet," he barely managed to say. Then he turned again to the man and asked him, "Will you be my servant?"

"'I should like to," the man replied. "But what would be my duties?"

"To ask me every now and then: 'For whom do you work?'"[7]

The servant was a living kavvanah. Whom will we get to ask us that question?

Slips and Errors

The most spiritual among us know that it is not only during our daily affairs that we may forget for Whom we work, Whose we really are. It may also happen in the very midst of doing a mitzvah, especially if the mitzvah becomes too familiar or too routine: ☞41

"The hasidim were once sitting together and drinking when the rabbi entered the room. It seemed to them that he was displeased. They said to them, "Are you unhappy to find us drinking, rabbi? Isn't it said that when hasidim sit together over their cups, it is just as though they were studying Torah?"

"There is many a word in the Torah," the rabbi of Rizhyn said, "which is holy in one passage and unholy in another. For example: it is written, and the Lord said to Moses, hew for yourself two tablets of stone, but also it says, you shall not make for yourself a hewn image. Why is it that the same word is holy in one passage and unholy in the second? In the first, the word "you" comes after, and in the second, it comes before. So it is with all we do. Where the "you" comes after, all is holy; when "you" comes first, all is unholy."[8]

That which elevates us can, if misused, bring us down. Raising our spiritual awareness through the medium of the material world - which is what the spirituality-of-the-everyday is all about - holds the danger of distracting us. We may end up looking at the finger instead of the holiness to which it is pointing. Or we may end up abusing the medium - working too much, drinking too much, even praying too much. Kavannah attentiveness can pull us back from such excess.

Focussing directly on other-worldly activities can be just as dangerous. A story about Rabbi Israel Salanter, the founder of the mussar (spiritual/ethical) movement of the mid-1800's, offers a warning this way:

"Once, on the eve of Yom Kippur, while on his way towards the House of Study for the evening prayers, Rabbi Salanter encountered a man who was known for his "fear of God." His face reflected fear and awe of the Day of Judgment, and his cheeks were covered with tears.

Rabbi Salanter stopped him to ask a question, but the man was so filled with fear of God that he did not answer him. Rabbi Salanter, in relating this later, said, "After I passed him, I thought to myself, Is it my fault that you are a God-fearing man and filled with trembling at the Day of Judgment? What has that to do with me? Are you not required to answer my question pleasantly and patiently, because such is the way of goodness and kindness?"[9]

God-wardliness is not an easy route to follow. Our righteousness can turn to revelry, or our piety can slip into incivility. And worse, we might never know it.

What strategies can we use to save us from these excesses? How can we help each other stay focused God-wardly?

38

How do you understand Heschel's concept of each spiritual act having three dimensions?

The spiritual pursuit, which is as natural to us as breathing, is at times so very hard to get right. With all the pitfalls, how are we to proceed? "The most one can do to achieve holiness is to make a beginning and to persist in one's efforts..."[10]

Each spiritual act, according to Heschel, has three-dimensions: the person, the idea and the audience of God.[11] We live spiritually not after or before or alongside of our daily activities, but through them.

Enoch was a cobbler, the hasidim tell us. And with every stitch of his awl he would say, "As I sew the upper soles to the lower soles, so may I bring the heavens above closer to the world below." It is not a matter of making time for spiritual living but rather making spiritual living part of our time.

Neither do we have to wait for perfection. We don't have to wait until we are without blemish and without doubt to pursue our spiritual quest. Religious living is not for the saints alone. If that were so, no one could stand before God. It is not perfection that we need to seek in our spiritual pursuits; not attainment. It is the courage and confidence to persist honestly and humbly in the pursuit itself.

An illustration of this is an incident involving world-famous violinist Yitzhak Perlman who was once performing at Avery Fisher Hall in Manhattan. He was in the middle of a solo when a string broke. As the audience of several thousand held its breath, Perlman almost instantaneously transposed the music he was playing, written for four strings, to a violin with three strings.

Afterward, when asked how he did this, Perlman who is known for his courage and fortitude with which he has faced the aftermath of polio, replied, "Sometimes you have to make music with what you have left."

According to that definition, we can all be musicians, playing the song of our spirit with the acts of our daily lives.☞<u>41</u>

EXERCISE 1: Proving the Existence of God

Write a letter to the editor of the local Jewish newspaper challenging the existence of God. What proofs will you bring? Next, write a response to that letter attempting to prove God's existence.

"God Does Not Exist:" _____

_____

_____

_____

_____

_____

_____

"God Does Exist:" _____

_____

_____

_____

_____

_____

_____

_____

How helpful has this exercise been for you?

_____

_____

40

EXERCISE 2: Everyday Spirituality

List ways in which you might be able to express your own spirituality through everyday actions.

_____

_____

_____

_____

_____

_____

EXERCISE 3: Spirituality Through Community

A constant goal of USY is to help its members gain a greater sense of spirituality and meaning in connection with God and other Jews. Write a letter to the leaders of USY and give them concrete suggestions as to how spirituality can be better expressed through the USY community.

_____

_____

_____

_____

_____

_____

_____

EXERCISE 4: Mitzvot and God

Debate the following statement:

"If a person performs a mitzvah but does not consider God when doing it, it is as if the mitzvah was not done at all."

EXERCISE 5: Defining Spirituality

Write your definition of spirituality

_____

_____

_____

_____

_____

_____

_____

_____

42

Chapter 3:
Belief and Suffering

Some of the greatest mysteries of life are wrapped in the darkness of pain, suffering and death

Why, we are all moved to ask, if God is all powerful, if God is good, if God cares about us, do we suffer?

This question has haunted us, and taunted us, from the time humans were able to rise above the way the world *is* to imagine the way the world *might be*. Many answers have been offered. Some people find comfort in one answer; others find comfort in another; and still others continue to rail against the night. Even after all these generations, we cannot say we have the answer.☞52

The Torah itself does not promise that we live in a perfect world. It teaches us that God created a world that is "very good." It is a world with love and health, kindness and caring, laughter and children, song and hope. But "very good" is not perfect, and in that slip between the two, the dark side of life thrives. So we see hatred and meanness, anger and illness, destruction and death.

Attempts at Understanding

What are some of the reasons given that try to help us to make sense of suffering and darkness? The very first attempt at an answer is found in Bereshit chapter 3: People suffer because people sin. Adam and Eve disobeyed God by eating the forbidden fruit. Even more, they tried to hide and deny their guilt. When questioned by God about his behavior, Adam replied: *"The woman you gave me gave the fruit to me and I ate it."* (Bereshit 3:12) Adam points his finger both at God and at Eve.

When questioned by God, Eve responds similarly, *"The snake deluded me and so I ate."* (Bereshit 3:13) If I am not blameless, both Adam and Eve seem to be saying, then at least you must see that I am a victim.

God rejects their answers. They have free will. They knew the rules. They disobeyed. They must take responsibility for their actions. In order to teach them this, God punishes them.

Adam and Eve's crime appears to be not only disobeying God, but refusing to accept responsibility for their actions. Can you think of examples in which individuals make a situation worse by refusing to own up to their wrongdoings?

44

This first effort to explain the existence of suffering, therefore, assumes that God is good and just and all God's acts are good and just. Humans are imperfect and disobedient. Moved by a commitment to justice, and a desire for us to be better, God punishes us. Pain is given in response to our wrongful actions. As Jeremiah says: *"Every one shall die for his own iniquity."* (31:30)

This approach preserves some precious beliefs: God is an active player in the world; God cares about us; God is just.

There are, however, two problems here:

Is it truly better for God to be more just than merciful? That is, must we be punished if we misbehave? Perhaps a firm "no," followed by a talk and a hug at the end might be a better response. Must our punishment fit our actions? Even if we must be punished, shouldn't our punishment be designed to turn us back toward God, to erase the distance, bring us closer together, rather than banish us? If not, there is no transformative or educational value to punishment. It is simply punitive.

Throughout the ages, Judaism rejected this argument for strict justice. As early as the book of Genesis, we learn that the world can be run, and in some cases should be run, according to ways of mercy. When God desires to destroy Sodom and Gomorrah for their immorality, Abraham intervenes:

> *Will You sweep away the righteous with the wicked. Perhaps there are 50 righteous persons there. Would you sweep away and not forgive the place for the 50 righteous persons that are there?... Shall not the judge of all the earth act justly?* (Bereshit 18:23-25)

God is moved and agrees that even if there are 10 righteous persons, the city will be saved.

There are two remarkable aspects to this story: Abraham's *hutzpah* in challenging God, and the way Abraham redefines justice. Justice, according to Abraham and adopted here by God, is not the cold formula of "sin yields punishment." Justice here must make room for mercy. Justice must make mercy a part of itself.

On the High Holidays we remind God of this definition, and ask that God move on this Day of Judgment from the seat of justice to the seat of mercy. For if God were all justice, who of us would live? Only when justice is tempered by mercy is there room for repentance and life.

What does it mean to say, "justice must make mercy a part of itself?" How would such a belief change what you do? Can a human court function with such a belief?

Our experiences do not always accord with this belief. Good people die young; wicked men prosper; evil nations dominate the world. How do we understand this?

Do we assume some hidden failing on the part of those who suffer? Doesn't that compound the pain: (1) for the "punishment" and (2) for the shame of others believing we did something wrong?

Our tradition has explored many other ways to explain why those we think are good suffer and those we think are bad do not. I offer some classic and contemporary answers:

We still are guilty.

Despite what we think, we must have done something wrong. Whether as individuals or as a people, if we suffer, it is a sign of our guilt. In the musaf amidah for the pilgrimage holidays, we recite these words: "Because of our sins we were banished from our land." This way of thinking tells us that we must have done something terrible to cause God to banish us from our land, even if we are not exactly sure what we did. When the Temple was destroyed, the rabbis explained it was due to *sinat hinam*, unfounded hatred between Jews. Sadly, there is always enough of that sin to blame any misfortune on.

God's justice can be delayed.

> *For the Lord of Hosts has ready a day against all that is proud and arrogant; against all that is lofty - so that it is brought low.* (Isaiah 2:12)

God does not operate by American principles of law. Justice delayed is not justice denied. The Eternal operates by a different standard of time. The ones who are evil will suffer later in life or in the afterlife. And the ones who are good will prosper later in life or in the afterlife.

The chosen suffer.

God loves us, the people Israel, as a parent loves a child. That means that we are held to high expectations. Our punishment (suffering) may exceed our misdeeds because of this love. God wants us to be our best, and do our best, and by punishing our minor missteps, God is urging us on.

Abraham Joshua Heschel once said: "We may not all be guilty, but we are all responsible." What do you think this means?

Is it possible for great evil to occur throughout a society due to the ways in which individuals treat each other?

It is often said that Judaism does not believe in an afterlife. While certainly not a primary focus of Jewish tradition, the rabbis did have some conception of a life after death. What do you believe happens after we die?

Bear in mind that the Lord your God disciplines you just as a man disciplines his son. Therefore, keep the commandments of the Lord your God: walk in His ways and revere Him. (Devarim 8:2-6)

According to this perspective, suffering has some educative value. It could perhaps be reworded by the saying "that which does not kill you, makes you stronger," or "suffering builds character." Do you agree or disagree?

46

It is not for us to understand the ways of God.

Job was a wealthy, successful God-fearing man, with a loving wife and many children. In a gamble with Satan over whether Job would still be God-fearing if he were less fortunate, God allowed Satan to do his worst. Satan killed Job's children, robbed him of his fortune, afflicted him with disease. Job's friends and wife offer varying explanations for why Job is suffering and what he should do about it. At the end of the book, after Job refused to accept responsibility for bringing on this suffering, the book offers the following remarkable answer:

> Then the Lord replied to Job out of the whirlwind: Who is this who darkens counsel, speaking without knowledge? ... Where were you when I laid the earth's foundations? Do you know who fixed its dimensions or who measured it with a line? Who closed the sea behind doors when it gushed forth out of the womb...? Have you commanded the day to break, assigned the dawn its place so that it seizes the corners of the earth and shakes the wicked out of it?... Does the rain have a father? Who begot the dewdrops? From whose belly came forth the ice? Can you send an order to the clouds or an abundance of water to cover you?.. (selections from chapters 38-40)

The questions continue until God falls silent, and Job replies:

> I know that You can do everything, that nothing You propose is impossible for You. Who is this who obscures counsel without knowledge? Indeed, I spoke without understanding things that are beyond me... I had heard You with my ear but now I see you with my eyes. Therefore I recant and relent being but dust and ashes. (Job 42:1-6)

God's ways are beyond our ability to understand. Better that we not try to understand them, for such an effort will lead us to falsehoods. Clearly, we construct explanations for ourselves, not for God. God does not need us to be God's advocate. Better we should be silent and humble than construct lies about God for our own comfort. Bad things happen. We should question them no more than we question the good. Sadness is no more mysterious than laughter; death no more stunning than birth. Why question one and rejoice at the other? As Judaism teaches us, we must bless God for the bad as well as the good.

The rabbinic and medieval periods expanded upon these approaches.

"From the opening verses we learn that Job suffers because Satan does not believe anyone can be as pious as Job and challenges God. This has never felt like a good enough reason for human suffering - someone is dying or bankrupt because God wants to prove a point.

We can learn two things from the Book of Job:

1) Job can approach God in the depths of his pain and is not sent away. God is approachable. God listens. God responds, although God's response may not be a satisfying one.

2) We do not suffer as a punishment. We learn lessons in compassion, in what to say and what not to say in the presence of someone who has fallen on difficult times. (We do not say "You must have done something wrong.")" - D.C.

Can you think of examples in which innocent victims are blamed for the evil that befalls them? According to this perspective, what would be a more reasonable means of reacting to people who fall victim to evil or misfortune through no wrongdoing of their own?

Yissurim shel ahava - Suffering that brings God's love

> *Rav Yossi son of R Yehuda said: "Welcome are sufferings for the name of God rests upon the one who suffers." Rabbi Natan the son of Rabbi Yossi said: "Suffering yields gifts from God."* (Sifrei Vetkhanan, piska 32, p 56)

This is a most puzzling view of suffering. It seems to accept the notion that we are not necessarily responsible for the pain that comes into our lives. It seems to also hold that God may or may not be responsible for our suffering. It might also be the case that God is not able to stop it. And yet, it teaches that God notices it, that suffering places us in the presence of God.

On the other hand, this belief might be saying that God does choose to cause our pain because pain is cleansing, and out of love God wishes us to be cleansed. But the common thread of "sufferings of love" is that God is with us when we suffer, and that God's presence itself is a gift and a comfort.

Suffering, especially death, atones for our sins and makes us worthy of receiving gifts from God.

> *Rabbi Shimon bar Yohai said: Precious are sufferings for on account of them God gave the Jews three good gifts, and they are: the Torah, the land of Israel and the world to come. (Mekhilta, ba-hodesh)*

Dying is seen as the ultimate suffering, and is seen as the ultimate atonement. *"If I die, let my death be an atonement for all my sins, misdeeds and iniquities. Let my lot be in Gan Eden and let me merit eternal life."* (Vidui - the confessional prayer) So Jews would pray when they were very ill. And such a prayer brought some comfort. For by atoning for all our misdeeds in this life, we have cleared the way to enjoy the glories of the afterlife.

Our suffering is unfair, so we challenge God.

> *"You have rejected and disgraced us;
> You do not go with our armies.*
>
> *You make us retreat before our foe;
> Our enemies plunder us at will...*
>
> *You make us the butt of our neighbors,
> the scorn and derision of those around us...*

According to this perspective, God is not viewed as a judge, but as a friend, comforting an individual in pain. Do you believe that there are any gifts to be found within suffering?

This notion of suffering emphasizes, as does the notion that God's justice can be delayed until the world to come, a belief in the afterlife. Do you believe that death might really be rebirth? Do you believe that what appears to be punishment, might instead be a gift?

48

There is a tradition within Judaism of challenging God's justice: Abraham challenges God because of God's desire to destroy Sodom and Gomorrah. Job challenges God for the evil that befalls him personally. Construct a scenario in which Jews challenge God's justice for an event or circumstance in contemporary times.

Some pain is not preventable. Disease and natural disaster are part of the natural order, the way in which God created the world. God is not responsible. Within this perspective, God is not viewed as judge. What might be a more fitting model for God according to this understanding of the reason for suffering?

All this has come upon us, yet we have not forgotten You, or been false to Your covenant. Our hearts have not gone astray, nor have our feet swerved from Your path, though You cast us, crushed us... and covered us with the deepest darkness...

Rouse Yourself, why do You sleep, O Lord?

Awaken, do not reject us forever.
Why do You hide your face, ignoring our affliction...

Arise and help us, redeem us as befits Your faithfulness. " (Tehillim 44)

Sometimes we are confident that no matter what anyone might say, we do not deserve to suffer so. If we believe that God has a hand in our daily affairs, then we must respond by challenging God. "This is wrong, God," the psalmist says, hoping to shake God into proper action. Perhaps God will respond as the psalmist wants; perhaps not. But at least this way the psalmist maintains his rightful sense of innocence, and his dignity. And when we suffer, these two may be the first to go.

Death and suffering are natural, if painful, limitations of the natural world.

We say that God acts in one of two ways: with *midat ha-din* or *midat harahamim.* These terms are most often defined as "the way of justice" or "the way of mercy." Rabbi Nancy Flam offers another interpretation: *midat hadin* is the natural law. It describes the necessary limits of the natural world. Physical bodies have boundaries and limits. We are created and without exception pass away. This is part of God's holy design. It is neither good nor bad. It simply is. *Midat harahamim*, the way of mercy, is not opposite the way of judgment, but a partner with it. Mercy softens the harsh edges of judgment. It is what enables us to endure justice, to hope beyond punishment, to care for each other through the pain.[1]

Suffering happens and God is with us.

Rabbi Harold Kushner wrote a best-selling book entitled <u>When Bad Things Happen to Good People.</u> It was his response to the tragic death of his young son. Rabbi Kushner does not believe that God caused his son's death. He does not believe that his son deserved to die. He knows that quite simply, and tragically, death happens, illness strikes, and God cannot stop this. But that does not mean God is absent when we suffer.

Rather, Rabbi Kushner believes that God is with us when we suffer, when we have the strength to carry on, when our neighbors and friends come to comfort us in the night, to bring us good food, to hold our hands, and to be with our families when we can't.

When people gather together with help and comfort, God is there.

In our suffering, God is there. In the laws of *bikkur holim,* visiting the sick, we are told not to sit at the head of the bed of the one we are visiting, for the Shekhinah hovers there. The rabbis tell us that God shares our pain: *"As one twin feels the other's pain, so God feels the pains of Israel."* (Pesikta de Rav Kahana).☞52

How We Can Respond

When we see suffering, our first impulse is to help the other. This is as it should be. For we are not only "our brother's keeper," we are also the hands and face of God. (This too is being a witness to God's concern.)

There is a joke which speaks of a man who was trapped in his house during a flood. His neighbors first sent him a raft, then a boat, and finally a helicopter to lift him away from the rising waters. He. refused them all saying, God will save me. Ultimately, he died in the waves of the flood waters.

When he went to heaven, the man stood before God and complained: "I believed in you my whole life. I prayed to you and was faithful. Why didn't you save me?"

And God replied, "I tried. Three times."

When we seek God in our times of need, we can find God through the help of others.

Sometimes, when others suffer, we cannot fix it. We cannot call back the accident, or restore another to health. But still there is something we can do. We can be with them, stay with them, hold them, and be witnesses to God's character of *midat harahamim.*

Suffering as a Pathway to God

Paradoxically, suffering - which is often seen as an obstacle to belief - can bring us closer to God. During illness and difficulty, we tend

---

Why, according to those who hold this belief, can God not help us?

Because God cannot tamper with the laws of nature?

Because God chooses not to tamper with laws of nature?

Because God chooses to preserve our free will?

Because God chooses to let humanity do God's work on earth?

Or is it because there is no God?

Do our answers serve God or us? Do they protect God or us?

Can we believe in a God who limits divine intervention when children die and murderers roam free? - Can we not believe in God? Which is better? Which comforts us more? How do we decide?

Faith ultimately is based on more than God's place in our suffering. God's place in our suffering is shaped by our faith. The one shapes the other.

50

to turn to God for help. *"Heal me, God, and I will be healed,"* we call out in the amidah. Every morning we recite these words: *"The Lord is present with the brokenhearted, and restores those who are crushed in spirit."* (Tehillim 34:19). Foxholes and hospital beds can be ladders to God.

"While other gates of heaven may sometimes shut, the gate of tears is never closed," the rabbis teach us.

We would not choose suffering as a way to draw closer to God. But if we suffer, when we suffer, it is comforting to know that **something of value may come of it.**

Why we suffer is a question we may never be able to answer. **How** we suffer (alone or with friends), and how we respond to suffering (broken or in dignity, in a way that brings comfort or pain to our loved ones, in a way that inspires or leads to despair), is in our hands.☞54

Something of value may come of it. This does not mean that we should believe that illness has purpose or meaning, that suffering is good, or that God sends us this or that disease as a message about how God wants us to live our lives. Not at all. But it does mean that suffering can open our eyes to lessons we otherwise are too busy or too self-satisfied to learn. We may learn that we need to spend more time with our families; that we have been valuing the wrong things; that others need us more than we knew; that the greatest pleasures in life lie not in what we can take, but in what we can leave: a healthy earth; a legacy of love; a tradition of rituals, acts and ethics that make life worth living.

Speaking the Unspeakable: Words About the Holocaust

One of the greatest challenges to God's existence and God's goodness is found in the experience of the Holocaust. How could God have let it happen? Even if we believe that God in principle does not intervene, how could God sit this one out?

So many have tried to answer this question. In the end, it is unanswerable. Some survivors came through their experience of the concentration camps with their faith strengthened. Some came through with their faith destroyed. Who is right? Sometimes even trying to answer feels blasphemous.

Elie Wiesel wrote a book called <u>Night</u> which speaks of his experiences in the Holocaust. In one scene he relates the story of a young boy who was hanged by the Nazis in the center of the camp. One Jew who was forced to witness this public horror turned to another and asked: "Where is God now?" And the other Jew answered: "He is there on the gallows."

When we are faced with a mystery, and we have no answers, and we cannot keep silent, we do the only thing we can: tell the story. Here is a selection from the story told by Dr. David Weiss Halivni, a talmudic scholar and Holocaust survivor:

> *When the sound of the closing of the door, after the first child was shoved into the crematorium, reached heaven, Michael, the most beneficent of angels, could not contain himself and angrily approached God. Michael asked, "Do You now pour out Your wrath upon children? In the past, children were indirectly caught up in the slaughter. This time they are the chief target of destruction. Have pity on the little ones, O Lord." God, piqued by Michael's insolence, shouted back at him, "I am the Lord of the Universe. If you are displeased with the way I conduct the world, I will return it to null and void." Hearing these words, Michael knew that there was to be no reversal. He had heard these words once before in connection with the Ten Martyrs. He knew their effect. He went back to his place, ashen and dejected, but could not resist looking back sheepishly at God and saw a huge tear rolling down His face, destined for the legendary cup which collects tears and which, when full, will bring the redemption of the world. Alas, to Michael's horror, instead of entering the cup the tear hit its rim, most of it spilling on the ground - and the fire of the crematorium continued to burn.[2]*

EXERCISE 1: Suffering

Have you had any personal experiences with the "seeming injustice of pain and suffering?" What were they? How did you feel when this was happening?

_____

_____

_____

_____

_____

_____

_____

EXERCISE 2: Why is There Suffering in the World?

On a scale of 1 (strongly disagree) to 10 (strongly agree), rate the degree to which you agree with each possible explanation for why there is suffering in the world. Explain your answer on the line after each explanation.

We still are guilty

1(strongly disagree)   2   3   4   5   6   7   8   9   10(strongly agree)

_____

_____

God's justice can be delayed

1(strongly disagree)   2   3   4   5   6   7   8   9   10(strongly agree)

_____

_____

The chosen suffer

1 (strongly disagree)   2   3   4   5   6   7   8   9   10 (strongly agree)

_____

_____

It is not for us to understand the ways of God

1 (strongly disagree)   2   3   4   5   6   7   8   9   10 (strongly agree)

_____

_____

Yissurim shel ahava - **Suffering that brings God's love**

1 (strongly disagree)   2   3   4   5   6   7   8   9   10 (strongly agree)

_____

_____

Suffering, especially death, atones for our sins and makes us worthy of receiving gifts from God

1 (strongly disagree)   2   3   4   5   6   7   8   9   10 (strongly agree)

_____

_____

Our suffering is unfair, so we challenge God

1 (strongly disagree)   2   3   4   5   6   7   8   9   10 (strongly agree)

_____

_____

Death and suffering are natural, if painful, limitations of the natural world

1(strongly disagree)   2   3   4   5   6   7   8   9   10 (strongly agree)

_____

_____

Suffering happens and God is with us

1(strongly disagree)   2   3   4   5   6   7   8   9   10 (strongly agree)

_____

_____

EXERCISE 3: Your Understanding of Suffering

Aside from the nine responses to suffering detailed in this chapter, do you have any other ways to understand suffering? If so, what is it?

_____

_____

_____

_____

_____

_____

_____

Introduction to Chapters 4, 5, & 6

Study, prayer and mitzvot form the classic rabbinic spiritual triangle. Since the time of the development of the Mishnah and Talmud, every observant male Jew has built his spiritual life on a webbing of these three behaviors. In different times and different places, different communities would choose one or another of the sides of the triangle as their favored way to spiritual fulfillment: the hasidim would stress prayer in joy; the **mitnagdim** study in earnest; the kabbalists the mitzvot done with the proper intent. But all three components would always be present for all groups. This has always been considered the Jewish way for men.

Women, for a variety of reasons - both chosen and imposed - possessed a different set of spiritual expressions, which scholars are just now uncovering. Just as the men had their body of knowledge, so the women had theirs: remedies and medicines for healing, traditions in childbirth and childrearing; prayers for the well-being of their family members (both living and dead); recipes and rituals for daily and holiday foods.

The women performed a host of social, philanthropic, holiday, and home-based "mitzvot" that wove together the fabric of family and communal life. In some communities, women's ways of Torah included reciting the classic daily prayers in addition to their own, and studying differing types of Torah-based texts (like the Tsena U'r'ena, a Yiddish retelling and commentary on the Torah written in the late sixteenth century for the Jew who did not know Hebrew and which became a favorite study-text of Jewish women). Altogether, Jewish women's religious behavior was rich, constant, renewing, authentic and rewarding for those who practiced it. Sadly, because it was largely practiced outside the arena and interest of Jewish men, it was for the most part neither formally acknowledged nor officially recorded. Much of it has been lost.

The spiritual expressions that are presented in the following three chapters represent a sampling of the classic ways of Jewish expression, including a modest appreciation of women's unique ways of religious expression. Over the years, as more information about women's ways of spiritual life is uncovered, and as both men and women continue to enrich contemporary ways of Jewish religious expression, these chapters will no doubt expand.

The opponents of early hasidism became known as **mitnagdim** (literally - those who are opposed). Their opinion was that hasidism's lack of emphasis on Torah study was a serious threat to Jewish life. The hasidim and mitnagdim were largely reconciled by the end of the 19th century.

Chapter 4:
STUDY

For most of our male spiritual ancestors, study was the premier and fundamental spiritual experience: "*Talmud torah keneged kulam*; the study of Torah is the foundation of it all."

It is not hard to see why. For those who see the Torah as "the word of God" handed to Moses, to study the Torah is to touch a bit of God.

For those who believe that the Torah is the record of the Jewish people's response to the **Revelation** at Sinai, the study of Torah is a sacred and exalted exercise, helping us stretch ourselves toward holiness and each other as we reach toward God.

For those who think that the Torah is a human creation, albeit the highest expression of the ways and wisdom of the Jewish people, studying Torah serves to connect them to the eternal soul, values and community of Judaism.

Why such emphasis on the study of texts? What happens when we study Torah?☞64

First a definition: "Torah" technically means the Five Books of Moses. But often when we say Torah, we mean so much more. We mean all the words and texts and law books and midrashim and stories that have been created in response to Torah. In this sense, the Bible is Torah, the Talmud and rabbinic commentaries are Torah, sermons are Torah, this book is Torah, and your responses to this book are Torah. We will use "the Torah" to refer to the Five Books of Moses, and "Torah" for everything else.

Now, a story:

Ben Azzai was sitting and expounding [the words of Torah] and fire surrounded him. [His students] went and said to Rabbi Akiba: "Rabbi, as Ben Azzai sits and expounds, fire burns around him."

Rabbi Akiba went and spoke with him: "I hear that when you teach, fire burns around you."

"Yes," he responded.

The Rabbis wondered what is greater: study or deeds. Rabbi Tarfon said deeds are greater. Rabbi Akiva said study is greater. They all agreed that study is greater for it leads to deeds. (Kiddushin 40b) What do you think?

Revelation literally means "the revealing." In this context, it refers to the moment on Mount Sinai when God pulled back the celestial curtain just a bit, just for a moment, to reveal a bit of God's self to the Jewish people.

Abraham Joshua Heschel said that Torah is a midrash on revelation.

Do you agree that your responses to this book are "Torah?"

58

"Were you perhaps delving into the secrets of the Chariot?" [the mysteries of the mystical texts which Akiba had mastered but which were dangerous for the uninitiated].

"No," Ben Azzai replied. "I was only making connections among the words of the Torah and from the Torah to the Prophets, and from the Prophets to the Writings and the words rejoiced as when they were delivered from Sinai, and they were sweet as when originally uttered." (Shir HaShirim Rabbah 10:2)

Torah comes alive when we become its partner, when we cradle its words, adorn them with our thoughts, and weave them together into our lifelines. For the words and letters of the Torah are unlike the words and letters of any other book. They both mean exactly what they say and what they never said before. They are both ink on parchment and black fire on white fire.

Rabbi Levi Yitzhak said: It is written in Isaiah: "For instruction shall go forth from me." What does this mean? The Torah was written in black letters, with the white spaces serving as symbols of teaching. It is just that we are not yet able to read these spaces. In time to come, God will teach us the white hiddenness of the Torah."

The Torah is an eternal, unchanging text which has to make sense in every culture and place. If it could not be both eternal and changing, it would have died and been forgotten years ago. It is a living tree, sprouting new growth with every mind that studies it, with every generation that nurtures it. It is a scroll, adding new sections while preserving the old ones.

The Torah is like a magic mirror, reflecting back to each reader what he needs to know, or what she can become. The young child reading the story of the binding of Isaac might wonder how he would have felt if he had been Isaac. A father reading the same story might wonder if he would have done what Abraham did. A mother reading the story might wonder where Sarah was.☞<u>64</u>

The midrash teaches the same lesson:

> *The Torah says: "In the third month after the children of Israel left the land of Egypt, on this day, they came to the wilderness of Sinai." Why does it say "on this day" and not "on that day?" The rabbis answer: Every day it is as if we receive the Torah anew."* (Rashi Shemot 19:1)

The Baal Shem Tov taught: "Teivah means ark, but also letter. When God commanded Noah to enter the ark, it was a sign that each of us must enter the sacred words of the Torah. Through the study of Torah, one enters the sacred word."

What would we lose if the Torah were not eternal? What would we lose if it were not changing?

"The Torah must be interpreted according to each generation's needs and according to the soul-root of those who live at that time"[1]

And not just new for each generation, but new for each individual, every day of their life, depending on their age, their needs, and their station in life.

Peshat and Derash

How does the Torah remain the same and yet yield new fruit for each generation? Through the interplay of **peshat** - the timebound meaning with which the text was written, and **derash** - the timeless meaning which the reader finds in it.

Bahya ben Asher of Saragossa wondered, "Why is the Torah written without vowels? So that the consonants may explode into sparks with many meanings."[2] Imagine the consonants symbolizing the *peshat* and the lack of vowels symbolizing the *derash*. The physical appearance of the Torah itself, then, contributes to this eternal/dynamic pairing. The writing yields innumerable interpretations. Without punctuation, the phrases rely on us to give them structure. Without vowels, the words rely on us to give them meaning.

Torah study is a gateway to the Garden of Eden, the timeless gathering place of the Jewish people. It is not reserved for a learned elite, but is accessible by all those who desire it.

> "A story is told about a rabbi who once entered Heaven in a dream. He was permitted to approach the temple of Paradise where the great sages of the Talmud, the tannaim, were spending their eternal lives. He saw that they were sitting around tables studying the Talmud. The disappointed rabbi wondered, Is this all there is to Paradise? Then, suddenly, he heard a voice say: You are mistaken. The tannaim are not in paradise. Paradise is in the tannaim."[3]

We carry the potential of eternal life within us. We carry the potential for peace and knowledge within us. We open the door to this potential when we open the covers of a **book of Torah**.

Torah and Partnership

With study, a Jew is never alone. When studying, a Jew always has two partners: God and all the Jews who ever studied that text.

One of the very first prayers we recite every morning praises God for sanctifying us through the commandment to occupy ourselves

When studying Torah, we often come across sections whose meanings are problematic or not immediately clear to us. In interpreting these sections, we can use either of two methods. **Peshat** is the contextual sense of what has been stated. **Derash** is any number of meanings we can find within the text.

A book of Torah. The title page in many classic rabbinic texts is drawn in the shape of a high vaulted gate. Why do you think that is?

60

with the study of Torah. Even more, it goes on to speak of God as our teacher of Torah: *"Blessed are You, God, who teaches Torah to your people Israel."*

God did not just give the Torah to Israel one time years ago, and then leave. God teaches us Torah, now, through the lessons, the prayers and the insights we experience every day of our lives. The Talmud tells us that the Shekhinah joins the company of Jews, not only where ten people gather in prayer, or where three gather as a court, or two share words of Torah but even where one studies alone.

In the paragraph before the Sh'ma, we ask God to teach us, to show us the way: *"For the sake of our ancestors whom You taught, graciously teach us, our Father, merciful Father...."* That is what it means to be chosen; that we are the people to whom God gave the gift of Torah, with the charge to discover its unfolding lessons and wisdom throughout time.

Rabbi Louis Finkelstein would say, "When I pray, I talk to God. When I study, God talks to me." For those who believe, the voice of God can be heard in the study of texts, mediated through the generations of Jews who helped fashion them. To study something is to struggle with it, respect it and ultimately have a relationship with it. This might be why Heschel said: "The unique attitude of the Jews is not the love of knowledge, but the love of studying."[4]

That is what is called *torah lishma*, study for the experience of study itself, and how it strengthens our relationship with God. "How should we understand *torah lishma*? Perhaps you will say: I will learn Torah so that I will be called "wise," or so that I can sit in the yeshiva, or so that I will live long. The Talmud tells us otherwise: study for the love of the Lord your God." (Siddur Avodat Yisrael)

This sentiment is alive today among Jews who are returning to Torah study, and is captured by this poem by Lee Hendler:

> **T**a sh'ma - come and study.
>
> **M**y eyes can scan the page for the familiar:
> the shape of a letter, the presence of a root
> whatever lets me know I am partly home -
> able to utter a neural sigh of recognition.
> "You I know."
> "You I have seen before."
> And I am hearing and seeing at once
> even though I am only reading and thinking.

Every morning we recite, "Blessed are You who has chosen us from among the nations, and given us the Torah...." How do you understand this blessing?

Rabbi Louis Finkelstein was the fourth president and Chancellor of the Jewish Theological Seminary of America from 1940-1972 and was a prolific scholar on the talmudic period.

Rejoicing in my disorientation
I grope toward Jerusalem.
A willing player in an ancient
game of Blind Man's Bluff.
I think I am getting somewhere
until Torah takes over.
Barely understood concepts play hide and seek with my brain.
I count to ten and shout my warning
but all the good ideas are already
hidden in the best places.
So I run as fast as my intellect will take me
searching even as I go
for the telltale signs of
passing.

The echo of phrase
the force of act
the sense of moment
the edge of symbol
the sweep of time
the thrust of word
the presence of God.

When I find the last
I cease to play.
Wild pleasure renders up full joy
as I forget where I end and God begins.
For a moment
we are both in the same place.
Studying Torah together.[5]

If to study as a Jew means to enter into a dialogue with God, it also means to become partners with all the past readers of the text. Most of Judaism's classic texts are printed with many voices on every page. The Tanakh is printed with generations of commentators accompanying the text. This is also the case with the Talmud, Shulkhan Arukh, and even many prayer books. As Jews, when we study, we find ourselves joining an on-going conversation that has roamed throughout the centuries, across the oceans, deserts and mountains.☞65

Rabbi Moses Hayyim Efraim of Sudlikow taught:

"Everything depends upon the interpretation of the rabbis... Until they interpreted it, the Torah was not considered complete, but only half-finished. It was the rabbis, through interpretation, who made the Torah whole...."[6]

62

When we study our sacred texts, God is only the first of our teachers. The rabbis throughout the ages are our teachers too. Indeed, without them, we would not understand Torah. Torah is a text of layers, the lessons of each generation piling high like transparencies, building and brightening a three dimensional image. Torah is not one layer but all layers. Each generation, including our own, is called upon to add its own layer to the image. And each layer, and each generation, becomes part of our sacred tradition.

Torah study, then, is about building communities of Jews. Torah study is done best when it is done together, in pairs, or small study groups called *hevrusas*, or *hevrutot*. And it is perhaps best, when such pairs and small groups gather in one room. Such study becomes then not just a dialogue over a sacred text, but a conversation within a very present community. Such study is not done quietly, but quite out loud.

Such study groups forge strong bonds of friendship. Partners flow between the roles of teacher and student. Each brings the wisdom of their own lives, intellect and temperament to share with the other. Week after week, sometimes day after day, partners gather, giving wisdom and receiving wisdom, testing ideas, tossing them aside, circling back and moving forward, entering and shaping each other's lives and minds. The text becomes the twine that binds these partners to each other, and to all the *hevrusas* that are, ever were and ever will be.

"*Asei lekha rav u'knei lekha haver,*" find yourself a rabbi and acquire for yourself a study partner. (Avot 1:6) Why "acquire?" Because we must commit to giving up something precious to us - our time, our passion, our attention, wisdom, even our opinion - in return for something equally precious.

Study and Healing

The power of study can offer even more than partnership and belonging. It can offer healing. Classically, when a friend or loved one is ill, Jews recite psalms and prayers, hoping for a recovery. More and more, Jews are creating study groups to offer comfort and hope for those in need of healing, both to the friends who study and the one who is ill. At houses of shiva, mourners are often comforted with divrei torah, offered by friends and family members around the times of services. At *shloshim*, the end of the extended thirty-day mourning period, families and communities may gather for study. Why is this comforting? Because study places the mourner, and the memory of the deceased, in the eternal stream of Jewish life. And it does this through a ritual of teaching which is thousands of years old, in the midst of a loving community, invoking the presence of God.

And when one is growing old and losing one's vigor, one's looks, and one's station in life, one's learning will always be a friend. Rabbi Nehorai said:

> *The only trade I taught my son was Torah, for all the other trades serve a person well only in their years of vigor... but Torah is different. It is good for a person in the years of their vigor and gives them a purpose and hope in their old age.* (Rosh Hashanah 82b)

Learned Jewish men, and increasingly women, whose strength and energy, but not wit or wisdom, fail in later life, find companionship and purpose in the study of holy books.

Torah Study Changes Us

Rabbi Israel Salanter, the founder of the **Mussar movement**, said that one should study Torah daily, not for the sake of acquiring knowledge, or even for the sake of doing mitzvot, but for the sake of being changed by it. For Rabbi Salanter, study is a way of growing, improving, reaching beyond what we <u>are</u> to what we <u>could be</u>.

We do that by allowing the text to enter us and work on us. An eminent scholar once approached Rabbi Mendl of Kotsk and boasted that he had gone through the entire Talmud. "So," the rabbi retorted. "You have gone through the Talmud, but has the Talmud gone through you."[7]

As we enter the world of Torah, we must allow the world of Torah to enter us. For then, the opportunities for true wisdom, comfort, and belonging will be ours.☞66

Increasingly, women are gathering to study, often monthly, to welcome the new moon. Texts about renewal, the upcoming holidays, and the promise of redemption blend with songs and movement and time for personal sharing and support. It is a place where the national and the personal, the communal and the individual, are woven into sacred time and space.

The **Mussar movement** began in the mid-19th century and had as its emphasis studying and living by the beliefs of Jewish ethical literature.

"Rabbi Moses Hayyim Efraim of Sudlikow taught regarding Shemot 25:8: 'They shall make me a sanctuary so that I can dwell in them.' This means that we must create a sanctuary within ourselves for God to dwell in. But how can we take God and make God dwell in us? The only way is through the Torah which is God's name, which is identical with God."

It is written, "The tablets were the work of God, and the writing was the writing of God, harut - engraved - upon the tablets" (Shemot 32:16). Do not read harut - engraved, but herut - freed. For the only ones who are truly free are the ones who occupy themselves with the study of Torah (Avot 6:2). What do you think this means?

EXERCISE 1: The Nature of Revelation

Explain the differences between the three different views of revelation:

1) The Torah is the word of God.
2) The Torah is the record of the Jewish people's response to the revelation at Mt. Sinai.
3) The Torah is a human creation, albeit still a holy document.

Which one most closely mirrors your opinion and why?

_____

_____

_____

_____

_____

_____

_____

EXERCISE 2: The Torah as a Magic Mirror

What Torah portion was read at your Bar/Bat Mitzvah? How was God present in that portion and in what way can its lessons reflect back to your life?

_____

_____

_____

_____

_____

_____

EXERCISE 3: Partners With Past Readers[8]

Below is a sample of a page of Talmud, along with explanations of the different sections on the page. How is the Constitution similar to and different from the Talmud, in terms of this same type of "on-going conversation" between the generations?

Name of Tractate

Number of chapter

Name of chapter

References to law codes: Mishneh Torah, Maimonides, 1135-1204; SeMaG, Moses of Coucy, 13th century; Tur, Jacob ben Asher, 1269-1343; Shulhan Aruch, Joseph Caro, 16th century.

Cross references to other parts of talmudic literature.

The column by the *binding*, whether left or right hand side, is the commentary of Rashi (Rabbi Sh'lomo Yitzhaqi, of Troyes, France, 1040-1105). Generally a "running commentary."

Biblical sources (notes compiled 16th century by Joshua Boaz).

Critical notes, Joel Sirkes, 1561-1640.

Additional commentaries of other traditions.

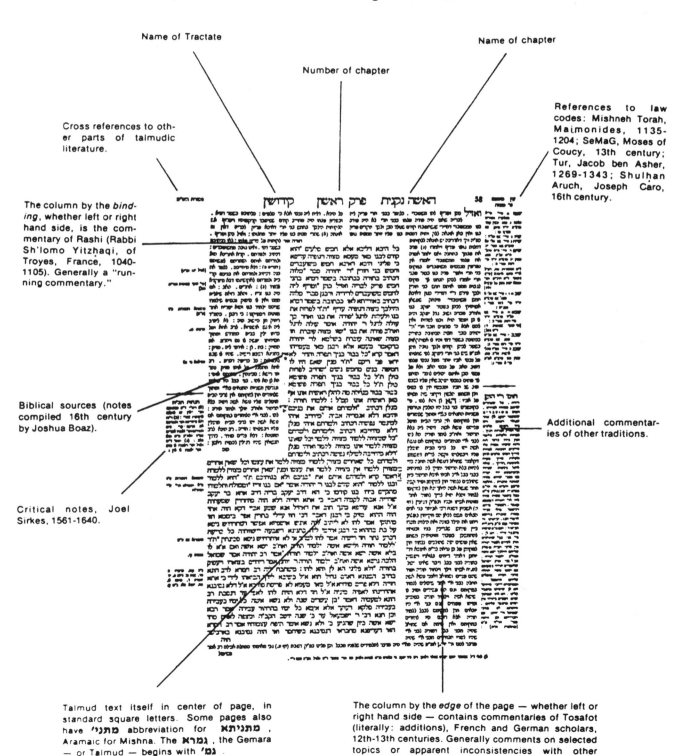

Talmud text itself in center of page, in standard square letters. Some pages also have מתני' abbreviation for מתניתא, Aramaic for Mishna. The גמרא, the Gemara — or Talmud — begins with גמ'.

The column by the *edge* of the page — whether left or right hand side — contains commentaries of Tosafot (literally: additions), French and German scholars, 12th-13th centuries. Generally comments on selected topics or apparent inconsistencies with other passages.

EXERCISE 4: Torah Study Changes Us

Can you think of ways in which you have been changed by the act of studying or something which you studied? What were the nature of the changes?

_____

_____

_____

_____

_____

Chapter 5:
Prayer

What is Prayer?

Nothing is quite so natural and irrepressible as prayer.

We humans, after all, are an expressive bunch. We like to share our feelings. When we are happy, we want to share the news with everyone we know (consider birthday announcements on ballfield score boards, and large wooden storks outside homes of newborns). For happiness is like laughter. The more we share it, the deeper it grows.

Likewise, when we are sad, we turn toward others, to tell our stories, to be held while we cry. For sharing our sadness allows it to drain from us, and creates an opening into which healing can flow. The rabbis tell us that when we visit someone who is sick, we take away one sixtieth of their illness. So it is with sadness. So it is with fear.

On most days, the words we speak and the tears we cry satisfy our immediate needs. But there are times, more often than we might admit, when our emotions overflow their boundaries. When our feelings overwhelm our everyday capacity for expression, when they are too great to be held by our listeners' hearts, we instinctively turn to the One who can receive, understand and hold us all.

Prayers of Petition

Our very earliest prayers, when we are still young, often well up from the springs of desire. They are likely to be prayers of request, when we innocently try to bend God's will to match our own. This is perhaps the most common form of prayer we utter throughout our lives: Please, God, let me do well on this test. Please, God, heal my mother. Please, God, don't let me be embarrassed. Please, God, let there be peace.

Judaism takes many of these sentiments and writes them into the prayers found in the siddur. A prayer against embarrassment, for example, is embedded in the announcement of the new moon ("Grant us a life, God, free from shame and reproach"). A prayer for healing is found in the *Amidah* ("heal us God and we will be

Prayer began as our need to speak spontaneously to God. Over the course of Jewish history, many of these prayers became set parts of our siddur. Obligatory prayer is a response to, and a boost for, spontaneous prayer.

68

Have there been moments in your life when you felt drawn to pray to God for something that was important to you? What was the prayer that you offered?

healed") and another can be said during the Torah reading ("May the One who blessed our ancestors Abraham, Isaac and Jacob, Sarah, Rebecca, Rachel and Leah, bless also this one, and restore him/her to perfect health...."). Personal petitionary prayers of all sorts can be added at the end of the amidah.

Human neediness blazes a trail toward God. But while neediness may be the first way to God, it is not the only way.

Prayers of Praise

Underlying these prayers of petition is our belief in, or at least desire for, the awesome power, presence and responsiveness of God.

> "I love the fact that God listens to my prayer and supplication. God bends an ear close to me. I will call to God all my days" (Tehillim 116:1).

Prayer is about awareness and wonder that leads from and flows to God. "The issue of prayer is not prayer," writes Heschel in his classic work on prayer, entitled Man's Quest for God. "The issue of prayer is God."[1] "To pray is to take notice of the wonder, to regain a sense of the mystery that animates all beings.... Prayer is our humble answer to the inconceivable surprise of living. It is all we can offer in return for the mystery by which we live."[2]

Prayer, according to Heschel, is not about what God *can give* to us, but about what God *has given* to us. And it is about what we in return can give God. It is not about wants and desires, but about amazement and appreciation.

According to one mystical school, "The world was created by the downward flow of letters: the task of man is to form those letters into words and take them back to God."[3]

> "Give praise to God, cry out God's name. Let God's great works be known among all peoples. Sing to God, give praise in verse, speak of all God's wonders." (Divrei HaYamim 1:17)

When we are overwhelmed by nature's beauty or awesome power, when we are amazed by the daily miracles of love, birth, life, and kindness, when we witness the blossoming of a rose, the restorative powers of medicine, and the brilliance of the human mind, we have an urge to turn toward God. We offer then not a prayer of obligation or petition. Rather, we offer a prayer about praying, like the sounds of a soft gasp of wonder. We might feel at such moments an unfiltered, unmediated attachment to God.

"Even if our mouths were filled with song as water fills the seas;

if joy could ride on our tongue like countless waves; if our lips could utter praise as limitless as the sky; and if our eyes could shine as radiantly as the sun.... never could we praise you enough, or thank you enough for all that you have done for our ancestors and for us." (Nishmat, from the Shabbat morning liturgy)

Even if our adoration were as large as God's creation, we could never satisfy our desire to praise God. Nor could we capture the fullness of God's grandeur. And yet we try. For a try in earnest is also a prayer.

A prayer of petition derives from a desire to bend God's will to ours. A prayer of awe derives from an impulse to sing the wonders of our Creator.

Prayer as an Expression of Love

Sometimes prayer is not about will or awe, but about expressions of love.

I betroth you to me forever; I betroth you to me in righteousness and in justice, in mercy and in kindness; I betroth you to me in faithfulness, and you shall know God. (Hosea 2:21-22)

This is what God promises the Jewish people in the Book of Hosea; and this is what we repeat every morning as we wrap ourselves in tefillin, our cosmic wedding band.

We recite the words daily both as a reminder of God's promise to us, and as a renewal of our promise to God. Bound together by this eternal bond of devotion, God and Jew seek to please each other, to fulfill each other's desire, to sing each other's praises. Not out of gratitude or manipulation or calculations of reciprocity (you do this for me and I'll do that for you). Rather out of rapture and joy, out of a desire to be with, do for and sing the praises of our beloved. So we recite *Ahavah Rabbah* every day:

"Deep is Your love for us, Lord our God, boundless your tender compassion. You taught our ancestors life-giving laws. They trusted in You, our Father and

"Prayer is a movement," says Naomi Rachel Remens, a doctor who helps those with cancer find a path toward healing, "from mastery to mystery."[4] What do you think that means?

Eliezer Berkovits says that we pray not to find answers, but to find God. "When there is nothing to hope for, one hopes for God alone. When there is nothing to expect, one deals with God alone. It is then that the confrontation between God and man reaches its ultimate culmination. One may still make God the confidant of one's sorrow, but instead of importuning, one accepts; instead of pleading, one praises."

70

King. For their sake graciously teach us. Father, merciful Father, show us mercy; grant us discernment and understanding. Then will we study Your Torah, heed its words, teach its precepts and follow its instruction, lovingly fulfilling all its teachings. Open our eyes to Your Torah, help our hearts cleave to Your mitzvot. Unite all our thoughts to love and revere you. Then we will never be brought to shame. For we trust in Your awesome holiness. We will delight in Your deliverance. Bring us safely from the four corners of the earth, and lead us in dignity to our holy land. You are the Source of deliverance. You have called us from all peoples and tongues, constantly drawing us nearer to You, that we may lovingly offer You praise, proclaiming Your Oneness. Praised are You, Lord who loves His people Israel. ☞ 80

And we in turn immediately recite about ourselves:

And you shall love the Lord your God with all your heart, and all your soul and all your might. (Devarim 6:5)

The eleventh century philosopher/theologian Bahya ibn Pekuda said in his major work on spirituality called Duties of the Heart: "Our sole object in prayer is the consummation of the soul's longing for God...."[5]

How Shall We Pray?

"There was a young cattleman who was unable to recite the Hebrew prayers. The only way he worshipped was by saying: 'Lord of the world! You know that if you had cattle, and gave them to me to tend, though I take wages for tending from all others, from you I would take nothing, because I love you.'" (Sefer Hasidim)

When we do not know the words of the tradition, we can speak the words of our heart. The earliest prayers in the Bible were, after all, prayers of the moment: *"Please, God, please heal her,"* (Bamidbar 12:13) Moses beseeched God on Miriam's behalf. And Hannah prayed: *"Lord of Hosts, look upon the affliction of your handmaiden, and remember me: give me a son, and I will dedicate him to the Lord all the days of his life...."* (I Shmuel 1:11)

Prayer can speak of love, but how can prayer lead to love?

But sometimes, the words of our heart fail us. They elude us or sound lame or empty or trite. At such times, we can turn to the words of our ancestors, brimming with tradition. When we take leave of a *shiva* house, we say, "May the One who is everywhere offer you comfort, amid all the mourners of Zion and Jerusalem". What could we think of ourselves that would be better? We say *shehekheyanu* when good times greet us, and we are overwhelmed with joy. We say *Barukh dayan ha-emet* when we hear of a death and we know not what to say.

Sometimes, however, our hearts are so full that all words fail us. At such times, all we have are tears. These too are prayers.

> *The people of Israel said, "We are poor. We have no sacrifices to bring as an offering."*
>
> *The Holy One replied: "I need only words, as it is written, "Take with you words" (Hosea 14:2) This refers to words of Torah.*
>
> *The people said: "But we do not know words of Torah."*
>
> *And God replied: "Weep and pray, and I will receive you."* (Shemot Rabbah 38:4)

Our tears can carry us to God.

Other times, all we have is silence: "To dwell in silence before God may also be counted as praying, for the root of prayer is neither informing God nor asking God; but in intimate reliance on God, making God the confidant of our heart."[6]

When We Can't Pray

As natural as it is to pray, it can often be difficult. Days, months, even years can go by without our experiencing the presence of God, without our experiencing that impulse to praise God's handiwork, or that confidence to make God our confidant. What do we do about prayer then?

Do we cease to pray, saying, "God is so far away. What good will it do to pray?" Or, "Why should I pray if it doesn't feel right?" Or, "God has turned away from me so I will turn away from God." Or, "I no longer believe there is a God."

And as day follows day without feeling God's presence, without holding the space for God - and prayer - to enter or re-enter our lives, we succumb to our habit of distance, to the silence that has fallen between us, to the feelings of emptiness, loss, atheism, anger, disappointment or abandonment.

Or sometimes we may try to pray again, challenging God to be there for us, but our prayers are met with silence. What are we to do then?

These are painful, even frightening thoughts, but they are not blasphemous. Almost every one of us has had them. And so have our ancestors.

> *My God, my God, why have you forsaken me? Why*
> *so far from delivering me? from answering my cries*
> *for help?* (Tehillim 22:2)

The psalmist too felt God's absence. And yet rather than withdrawing and waiting for God to reappear, the psalmist chose to reach across the gulf, to speak a prayer about the distance between them, in spite of the distance between them. Paradoxically, God's absence made God real to the psalmist. The psalmist does not ask, "I wonder, I wonder, is there a God?" but rather, "My God, My God, what are you doing?"

In the very act of throwing God-ward the words that reflect the psalmist's isolation, the isolation is broken. The burden and opportunity of continuing the relationship falls on both sides. As long as one side keeps it alive, it is alive; not vibrant and healthy, but alive. And as long as the relationship breathes, it can be restored. The poet Yehuda Halevi wrote:

> "Where will I find you, God?... I sought Your
> nearness, with all my heart I called to You, and when
> I went out to call for You, I found You, coming to call
> for me."

Prayer - even forced prayer and empty prayer - holds the space in our hearts, the place in our daily lives, where we once met God, and can meet God again. At such times, prayer is a marker, a prod, a reminder, a rehearsal, even a vehicle which can work to bring us closer to God and God closer to us. At such times, prayer is not a response to our awareness of the presence of God but an act of defiance when facing the absence of God.

As Mordecai Kaplan puts it: "Religious prayer is the utterance of those thoughts that imply either the actual awareness of God, or the desire to attain such awareness."[7] Prayer does not require belief, but hope.

Rabbi Nahman of Bratzlav tells us how to offer prayers from a distance:

"Make it a habit to seclude yourself in prayer, expressing your thoughts before God each day. If all you can say is a single word [due to doubt or confusion or distraction], repeat it over and over again. Even if you spend many days repeating this word, it is good. Repeat the word innumerable times. God will eventually have mercy and open your lips so that you will be able to express yourself."[8]

When Prayer Becomes Routine

Distance is not the only impediment to prayer. Paradoxically, in its own way, excessive intimacy dulls the ability to pray too. The constant, daily approach to God tends to make the extraordinary common, and tends to dull our response to prayer.

A Christian woman seeking closeness to God went to a monastery for nine months on a religious journey. Her experience is much like that of many Jews: "I learned that when you go to church several times a day, every day, there is no way you can [always] do it right. You are not always going to sit up straight, let alone think holy thoughts. You're not going to wear your best clothes but whatever is not in the dirty-clothes basket. You come to the Bible's great book of praises [she was **"davvening"** the psalms as we davven from our siddur] through all the moods and conditions of life, and while you may feel awful, you sing anyway."[9]

Daily davvening may dull the ecstasy of prayer, but it compensates through the comfort of routine, and community. God becomes at such moments not the majesterial and fearsome King of King of Kings, but our constant companion. God becomes the One who sewed clothes for Adam and Eve, the One who sets the table before us in the presence of daily life, the One who sees us in our jeans and hospital gowns, who knows us when we are grouchy and cross, who encourages us when we are too tired to try again.

Heschel too admits that routine and familiarity are impediments:

> "I am not always in a mood to pray. I do not always have the vision and the strength to say a word in the presence of God."

Davvening is the Yiddish word for praying or worshipping. Some people prefer to use this term when discussing the active roll of praying because it connotes a feeling of closeness and intimacy with God while praying.

To let silence awkwardly build among intimates, to let fatigue, lack of newness, boredom, or failure of imagination dull a relationship, can be just as damaging as silence due to feelings of distance and abandonment. Heschel offers his antidote:

> "But when I am weak, it is the law that gives me strength; when my vision is dim, it is duty that gives me insight."[10]

For Heschel, when the personal impulse to pray waned, the obligation to pray buoyed him. To many, the words of the codified liturgy and the thrice daily obligation to pray are seen as burdens, barriers set between themselves and God. For others, the liturgy is a precious heirloom which - at times when their words fail them - keeps that connection between God and them open. It is like that weekly call from our grandparents just to check in, even when we have nothing to say. It is our "good morning," "good night," "how are you," "fine thank you." It is all the practice swings we take, the scales we play, the speeches we rehearse. These rituals hold open the space between us and God when we have nothing else to say. When the time is right, the conversation will begin again, enlarged and deepened.

Rabbi Israel Friedman, the Rizhiner, tells the following tale:

"There was a small Jewish town, far off the main roads of the land. It had most everything it needed: a bathhouse, a cemetery, a hospital, and law court and all sorts of craftsmen. Yet one craftsperson was missing: the watchmaker. In time, many clocks became inaccurate and their owners stopped winding them. But others thought that no matter how inaccurate, as long as they ran, they should wind their clocks. One day, as fate would have it, a watchmaker came to town. Everyone rushed to bring him their clocks. But the only ones he could repair were those that had been kept running - the others had grown too rusty."[11]

Prayer may be either speaking to God, or holding the space, or rehearsing the muscles that will once again enable us to speak to God.

And the surprise about prayer is that sometimes when we enter into it out of obligation, we find it enters us, and fills up the space we have reserved for it.☞<u>81</u>

Private Prayers

Some prayers are private, recited in the singular, whenever we desire. The psalms are full of such prayers:

> *Sing to the Lord my soul; for the Lord my God is very great; You are robed in grandeur and glory.* (Tehillim 104:1)

> *Like a hart searching for water, my soul searches for you, God. My soul thirsts for God, the living God. When will I come to appear before God?* (Tehillim 42:2-3)

> *Hear my prayer, O Lord, give ear to my cry, do not turn away from my tears....* (Tehillim 39:13)

We find personal prayers in segments of the Talmud and in prayerbooks throughout the ages. The closing paragraph of the amidah ("My God, keep my tongue from evil and my lips from speaking lies.") is a private prayer that the amora Rav (3rd century, Babylonia) used to say. The amidah has at least two places within it where private prayers are encouraged: at the end of the amidah, and in the *refaeinu* prayer for healing. *Siddur Sim Shalom* helps us by inserting a reminder and a guide telling us that we may add this prayer on behalf of someone who is ill:

> "May it be Your will, Lord my God and God of my ancestors, that you send perfect healing, of body and of soul, to _____, along with others among the people Israel who are stricken."

Women have recited private prayers for generations, when they lit their Shabbat candles, went to the mikveh, entered pregnancy, labored, delivered and nursed a child.

> "Dear God, may it be your will that you provide nourishment for your humble creation, this tiny child, plenty of milk, as much as he needs; give me the patience to nurse calmly, as long as he needs. Cause me to sleep lightly so that the moment he cries I will hear and wake up. May the words of my mouth and the meditations of my heart be acceptable to you."[12]

Even today in some prayerbooks we can find standardized versions of the private prayers that women said over candlelighting:

What are some of your private prayers? Do you think that any of them can help others who might find themselves in the same situation? Consider writing them down. You may want to share them one day.

"There is a tension within the Jewish tradition between the needs of the individual and the needs of the community. Although most prayers may be recited alone, there are some elements which cannot be proclaimed without a minyan. Indeed, mourners and marriages require community.

And yet it would be inaccurate to say that there is no strong tradition of individual prayer. Indeed, there are even stories in the hasidic tradition that suggest that we have an obligation to go out to the fields and forests alone and to seek God. Have you ever davvened by the shore or in the woods? Listened to the music of the world around you? Sought God in the power and rhythm of nature? Praised God with the words of the daily prayers while feeling God's presence in the sunlight on your back?

Rabbi Nahman of Bratzlav wrote:

"Master of the universe, grant us the ability to be alone: may it be our custom to go outdoors each day among the trees and grass, among all growing things, and there may we be alone, and enter into prayer.

There may we express all that is in our hearts, talking with the One to whom we belong. And may all grasses, trees, and plants awake at our coming.

Send the power of their life into our words of prayer, making whole our hearts and our speech." - D.C.

"May it be Your will, Lord my God, that you shower kindness upon me [and my husband, children, mother and father] and all my family; and may You grant us and all Israel good lives and long lives... may you bless us with great blessings and make our homes complete. Please God, listen to my plea, in tribute to our matriarchs Sarah, Rebecca, Rachel and Leah, and may our light never be extinguished."

In any language, at any time, in any way, when our heart moves us, we can pray our private prayers.

Communal Prayers

Liturgical prayer, on the other hand, is communal prayer: it is said mostly in the plural, in Hebrew, and at set times.

No matter what our personal situation, no matter what our politics or tensions or historic conditions, the Jews are one people, God's people. God betroths all of us with verses from the prophet Hosea. We can feel God's distance or closeness as a people, as in the time of the Holocaust, or the creation of the State of Israel, or the daring rescue at Entebbe. Private prayer is the voice of the individual. Liturgical prayer is the voice of the community. We say: *"Blessed are you, Adonai, our God, Ruler of the Universe, who commands us to fill ourselves with words of Torah."* Were we really commanded? You and me? Yes, tradition tells us, because every one of the Jewish people was commanded years ago.

"The Bible is the record of God's revelation to Israel," Solomon Schechter once said. "And the siddur is the record of Israel's self-revelation to God." God reveals God's self to us in the Torah, this belief holds, and we reveal our hopes, our fears, and our passions to God through the pages of the siddur. Each partner in this intimate covenant feels the right, the desire and the duty to tell the other of their longings, their needs and their desires. And because the relationship continues, the siddur is constantly growing. The old prayers are our heirlooms, reminding us of the relationship our grandparents and their grandparents before them had with God. The new prayers renew the relationship.

In communal prayer, each of us is a surrogate for the whole. When we speak in the plural, we carry the weight and enjoy the support of the whole people Israel, whether we pray in a minyan or davven alone. The presence of our community is carried in the words of the siddur. Davvening from it we are never alone. When we lack words and feel far from God, others can speak to God on our behalf. When others find themselves adrift, we can carry them with our prayers.

To be a Jew is to never be alone. We are always part of our people. Alongside our private joys and fears, songs and sadness, we attach ourselves also to the joys and fears, songs and sadness of our people. Daily prayer keeps us attuned to the breathing, the pace and the emotions of our people. This attachment reminds us that each of us is more than the bundle of our own personal needs and desires; that our boundaries extend to the boundaries of our people. We are wagons in a caravan; cars on a passenger train. We are joined in our journey to our fellow-travelers. We move with them and they move with us. We are safer and stronger in the shelter of each other than we are alone. We may live our individual lives in the privacy of our domains; yet we share in the destiny of our fellow travelers, and they share in ours. Their presence gives us greater meaning, defines our space, and determines our language.

When we enter the synagogue we say: *"Ma Tovu Ohalekha Yaakov Mishknotekha Yisrael - How goodly are your tents, O Jacob, your dwelling places, O Israel."* (Bamidbar 24:5) The synagogue is the common dwelling place for all Israel, the roof which encompasses all our singular dwelling places. It is the place where we all belong, where we all have the same name - B'nei Yisrael.

Liturgical prayer teaches us this. It is a grand lesson in humility. Paradoxically, by putting words into our mouths, it "frees [us] from the tyranny of individual experience...."[13] To focus overly much on ourselves, as we are wont to do in western society, is to make out of our experiences a cage for our lives. We are never so lonely as when we become the center of our own concerns. If we are constantly caught up in our needs, we have no room for others, and they, caught up in theirs, have no room for us. Liturgical prayer frees us to be more than we are, and to care more than we otherwise might.

What Does Prayer Do?

Knowing the ways of prayer is to know that praying changes us. We may enter prayer agitated and upset, but the words and melodies of the prayers, and the presence and comfort of the voices of our fellow davveners may soothe us, and give us strength. We may enter prayer sad and lonely, but the place and words of prayer may remind us we are not alone.

There is a saying that goes: "Max goes to shul to talk to God. I go to shul to talk to Max." Going to shul to talk to Max is not beside the point, but part of the point.

"Prayer cannot mend a broken bridge, rebuild a ruined city, or bring water to parched fields. Prayer can mend a broken heart, lift up a discouraged soul, and strengthen a weakened will."[14]

But, prayer can only give to us, when we give ourselves to prayer. We must be open to receiving its power and its messages, open to its ways and wonder. The prayers are not so much ours, then, as we become the prayers.

There is a midrash which speaks of God praying. The rabbis ask: And what does God pray for? God says, "May it be my will that my passion for mercy overrule my passion for justice." Why does God pray? To affect God's self. Prayer acts upon the one who prays.

Prayer is about change, moving us more than moving God. This happens when we step out of ourselves through the words and ways of prayer, and see what we are otherwise not able to see. "Our supreme goal [in prayer]," Heschel teaches, "is *self-attachment* to what is greater than the self rather than *self-expression.*"[15] Self-expression turns us inward; self-attachment turns us outward.

Prayer Changes the Pray-er

"Prayer is a step on which we rise from the self we are to the self we wish to be...." It is a mirror which shows us both what we are and what we can become.

The root of the word *tefillah*, prayer, is **p.l.l.** It embraces a cluster of meanings: differentiate, clarify, judge, separate, distinguish, and discern, all necessary to the enterprise of prayer. To pray, in Hebrew, is לְהִתְפַּלֵּל - l'hitpalel, a reflexive verb which means we turn the act on ourselves. To pray then is to carefully and honestly see oneself, assess one's actions as objectively as possible, both for the good and the bad. Thus, says the author of Siddur Avodat ha-Lev, "Prayer is the soul's yearning to define what truly matters and to ignore the trivialities that often masquerade as essential." Prayer can be hard but invigorating. It puts us in charge of ourselves and gives us the tools to chart our lives.

Often it is precisely the routine aspect of our prayers that leads us to such renewal. Many people are most creative, can reach the deepest and purest parts of their mind, not when they focus directly on a creative task, but precisely when they don't. That is, when they are driving, taking a shower, or doing dishes, routine tasks that when done day after day occupy the mind and body but leave the

---

Why do <u>you</u> pray?

p.l.l. feels like the word "pull" in English, and the meanings in fact are not so different. Prayer helps us gently pull apart the complex feelings we have in our hearts and souls, so that we can view them better, know them better and judge them better. Prayer helps us stretch ourselves, open ourselves, so we can separate from the mold that has us trapped.

soul free to wander, thoughts of depth and connection have room to surface.☞81

For the Hasidim, like for Heschel, the purpose of prayer is to attach oneself to God. Prayer even more than study, is their premier path to God. But praying well requires discipline. And discipline requires constancy. So the hasidim teach that we should find not only a fixed time for prayer, but also a fixed place. Derekh Moshe writes:

> "Choose a fixed place for yourself, a place that is nice and clean and say out loud in a full voice, I choose this place for prayer for myself, my family and all Israel. May it be your will that the Shekhinah rest on this place as it does in all the synagogues of Israel."[16]

By returning to the same place day after day, we transform that place into holy space, and we become transformed when we enter it. Such is the power of dedication and habit.

Alone or in a group, sorrowful or proud, prayer weaves together the triangle of our lives: ourselves, our community and God.

What if I don't believe? What if I can't, or won't, or am stopped? Is there is a place for me in prayer? Prayer is a product of the human spirit, reaching toward the divine, that is, reaching toward the very best there is, the very best we can be. It is written in a language of symbols and images that build community, establish values, and reinforce hope. Prayer works not only because people believe in God, but because people also believe in each other. Prayer is the personal and communal expression of where we have been, and where we want to go, crafted in the language of God. God can be real for me, or God can be a symbol. Either way, prayer can embrace me and I can embrace prayer.

EXERCISE 1: Prayer as a Relationship With God

Not always do we pray for something in particular, but rather as a response to God. Upon being overwhelmed by the awesomeness of God's creation, or by the goodness with which we have been blessed, we may offer a prayer.

Read the text of Ahavah Rabbah (which can be found on pages 69 - 70), from the Shacharit (morning) service, and concentrate on the different ways in which love is mentioned. Also, think about the intricacies of love and how difficult it is to create a healthy, loving relationship. Finally, take a few minutes and quietly contemplate someone or something that you love. Next, write a personal love letter to that person or object which you have been contemplating.

_____

_____

_____

_____

_____

_____

_____

_____

_____

_____

_____

_____

EXERCISE 2: The Need for Fixed Prayers

Within Judaism, it is important that prayer be recited, not only at moments when we feel moved to pray, but as a discipline, three times each day. List some reasons why it might be important and worthwhile to pray, even when we do not feel the need or desire to do so?

_____

_____

_____

_____

_____

EXERCISE 2: The Routine of Prayer

When do you make your best decisions? When listening to music? Taking a shower? Why? How could prayer help you make decisions?

_____

_____

_____

_____

_____

82

Chapter 6:
Mitzvot

"In this world, music is played on physical instruments, and to the Jew, the mitzvot are the instruments by which the holy is performed."[1]
(Abraham Joshua Heschel)

Mitzvot are deeds that God asks us to do: Keep the Sabbath; honor your parents; care for the needy; tithe your produce; do not cut down fruit bearing trees. The original catalogue of mitzvot, found throughout the Five Books of Moses, is one of the key defining elements of Judaism.

According to the Torah, our doing the mitzvot pleases God and brings us rewards. In the second paragraph of the Shema we read:

If you earnestly attend to my mitzvot that I give you this day, to love the Lord your God and serve Him with all your heart and all your soul, then I will nourish your land according to its season - with autumn showers and spring rains - and you will have ample harvests of grain and wine and oil....

But take care lest you be tempted to forsake God and turn to false gods... for in wrath God will turn against you and close the heavens and hold back the rain. The earth will not yield its produce, and you will disappear from the good earth that God is giving you.
(Devarim 11:8-17)

What is the power and value of mitzvot? Why would God have stressed them so, and why do we continue to cherish and perform them?

Mitzvot Are a Gift of Love

Rambam, in one of his discussions on the reasons for obeying the law, writes:

A man must not say, "I will fulfill the commandments of the Torah, and I will devote myself to the study of its wisdom, so that I may obtain all the blessings which are written therein, or that I may attain unto

84

the life of the world to come...No, it is by no means becoming to serve God after this manner, for he who serves God thus does so out of fear, and consequently will never reach the state of the prophets or of the wise...[Rather] he who serves God out of love devotes himself to the study and to the performance of the divine commandments, and walks in the paths of wisdom not for the sake of any worldly advantage, nor because he fears evil, nor because he wishes to attain the bliss [bestowed upon] the righteous. He abides by its truth solely because it is truth, and good results will naturally follow.[2]

According to Rambam, we should observe God's commandments because **(1)** we love God, and **(2)** because God's mitzvot are true.

(1) When we love someone, we do what they want because that makes them happy. Not for reward, not for gain, but simply because it brings them pleasure. When such giving satisfies our beloved's desires, it satisfies ours as well. This kind of giving strengthens our love. That is why the tradition tells us: "Greater is the one who is commanded and performs a mitzvah than one who is not commanded and performs a mitzvah." America teaches us that volunteerism, that is, choosing to give when we want, the way we want, because we want, free of any compulsion or obligation, is the greatest demonstration of kindness and caring we could offer. After all, we need not give or act at all, but we do, out of our own free will.

Jewish values are different. In Judaism, the greatest act of philanthropy is not to give when we want, what we want and how we want, but to give when, what and how the other wants.

The mitzvot are what God desires of us. Therefore, we do them, as a gift of love.☞<u>92</u>

(2) As expressions of God's will, mitzvot are more than whimsical desires of our Beloved. They come from God, the author of truth; therefore, they are true and match the ways of reason. That in itself is motivation enough to observe the mitzvot. For, according to Rambam, the pursuit of truth and the conduct of reason offer their own rewards.

Moreover, each mitzvah has its own value. Each teaches us a special lesson. For example, the mitzvah of sending the mother bird away from her nest before taking her babies teaches us that animals too experience the parental feelings of love and loss. We should

Rabbi Lawrence Kushner suggests that we think of worship as more than reciting tefilot three times a day. He suggests that we consider the performance of mitzvot as another kind of worship, just as Heschel did when he marched in Selma. For when we perform mitzvot, we turn ourselves to God.

Observing the mitzvot is viewed by Jewish tradition as our gift of love given to God. Can you think of examples in which observing God's commandments was a gift from you to God, indicating your love for God?

What kinds of rewards do you receive for the "pursuit of truth?"

Have there been any times when you have learned a particular lesson from observing a mitzvah?

therefore avoid causing them undue anguish. The mitzvah of unloading the burden of an animal of someone you hate comes to teach us compassion, both for the animal and for the owner, even though we dislike him.

The mitzvot are the rays of light that burst forth from the prism of Torah hanging on the window of the world before us. God's will is the light, too brilliant for us to appreciate directly. The prism - the Torah - refracts God's will into segments that we can understand and absorb. They flood our world with color and purpose - the mitzvot.

Mitzvot are a Ladder Toward Godliness

Not everyone agrees with Rambam. Some classic Jewish thinkers believe that mitzvot have meaning not so much one by one, but only when taken together, as a body of **halakhah**. One particular mitzvah therefore, might, on its own, be meaningful or not. But embedded in a system of 612 other commandments, it is part of a ladder toward godliness.

There are, in our system of mitzvot, two kinds of commandments: ritual commandments (those that are performed between the individual and God, *mitzvot bein adam la'makom*) and moral commandments (those that we do as one person to another, *mitzvot bein adam l'havero*). In the first category fall the mitzvot of kashrut, Shabbat candlelighting, sacrifices and the like. In the second fall the mitzvot of burying the dead, paying a worker fairly and promptly, and giving tzedakah.

To the modern thinker, the whole system of mitzvot may seem irrelevant. After all, such a thinker might argue, the ritual commandments are irrational or nonsensical; the moral commandments self-evident and redundant. (That is, they can be learned through common sense and contemplating what is good.)

The **amora Rav**, who lived 1800 years ago, asks and answers the first part of this very modern question:

> *Does it really matter to God whether one slaughters an animal across the throat or across the back of the neck? [No, is his unrecorded reply.] Rather, the mitzvot were given for the purpose of refining human beings.* (Bereshit Rabbah 44:1)

Halakhah, which literally means, the walking, is a term used for (1) the collective body of mitzvot, (2) the system which guides the interpretation of the laws of mitzvot, and (3) a particular mitzvah.

The **amoraim** were the sages of the Talmud who were largely involved with interpreting the Mishnah and the non-legal aspects of the Torah [aggadah]. **Rav** founded the Sura Academy, which would flourish for 800 years from its beginning in 219 C.E.

86

Why do human beings need to be refined? Why weren't we created "perfect" to begin with?

There is a mistaken notion abroad in the land that the more "religious" one is, the more strict in observance one is. That is, many people believe that those who say no to halakhic possibilities are more religious than those who say yes; that one who interprets the Law narrowly is more religious than one who interprets it broadly. That is not so.

We do not become more religious or more holy by creating more restrictions for ourselves or our community. Remember that the *nazir*, the biblical ascetic who voluntarily gave up permissible behavior and comforts of life, was frowned upon in Jewish tradition. God's mitzvot yield holiness because they come from God. Mitzvot say what we *should do* as well as what we shouldn't do. Man-made stringencies that chip away at what we *can do* diminish the arena of God-given holiness.

How so? Halakhah infuses almost every one of our waking hours with guides to behavior. When we rise, halakha asks us to turn our thoughts to morning prayers, the wonders of the body, and the wearing of ritual clothing. We can orient our words, our thoughts and even our choice of clothes to the purpose of pursuing holiness. We say the prayers that are matched to the Jewish reckoning of time. In doing so, we remind ourselves that we belong to the community that counts time as we do, even if we live in the United States, or Canada, or anywhere else in the world.

When we prepare our breakfast and lunch for the day, we can turn our thoughts to permitted and forbidden foods, and permitted and forbidden combinations of foods and utensils. When we greet our friends, co-workers, strangers, we must strive to treat them with the dignity deserving of those created in the image of God, and strive to use language that avoids denigration or embarrassment.

Without halakhah, we would live our daily lives on a two dimensional plane, seeing the world as a picture, with height and width but no depth. With halakhah, every act we perform is hallowed by a third dimension. We are able to reach beyond the act itself, through the act itself, to the holiness that underlies, and unites, all life.☞92

By performing ritual commandments with the self-consciousness they demand, we connect our acts to the eternal stream of holiness. By transforming acts of goodness into acts of holiness, we reach beyond our own sense of right and wrong and join hands with the sacred source of the universe.

As Heschel puts it: "Ritual acts are moments which a person shares with God, moments in which a person identifies with the will of God."[3]☞93

Heschel teaches us an important lesson here. On the one hand, there is God: awesome, spiritual, eternal. On the other hand, there are humans: frail, material and mortal. How do the two communicate, or bridge the gulf? What language do we have in common? How do we penetrate the divide? In Judaism, the answer is: mitzvot. It is where God and Jew meet.

> "[A symbol serves] as a *meeting place* of the spiritual and the material, of the invisible and the visible. Judaism, too, had such a meeting place - in a qualified sense - in the Sanctuary. Yet in its history the point of gravity was shifted from space to time, and instead of a place of meeting came a *moment of meeting;* the meeting is not in a thing but in a deed."[4]

The clock at the train station may only tell us the time; but it becomes a symbol and source of meeting when we say, "Meet you there at 5:15." So it is with kiddush and tzitzit and mezuzot. They are the medium, the how, where and when of meeting godliness.☞93

And through this meeting, which lasts but a moment, a touch of the divine rubs off on us. That is what we call holiness. This holiness yields life's third dimension, connecting us beyond time and space to those who came before us, those who surround us, those who come after us, and the One who gives meaning to all. Perhaps this is the sentiment that underlies the following midrash:

> *"You shall be a holy nation."* (Shemot 19:6): A holy nation: what does this mean? Learn from what it says in the verse, *"You are a holy nation to God"* (Devarim 14:2). This refers to the holiness [that comes from] the mitzvot. For every time the Holy One gives the people Israel more mitzvot, he gives them more holiness. (Midrash Hagadol)

The moral commandments lead us to more than a life of morality. They lead us to a life of holiness.

> *'To walk in all God's ways.'* [How can humans walk like God? the midrash asks.] These are God's ways, as it says: *'Adonai, Adonai, God of compassion and mercy, slow to anger, full of kindness and truth, extending caring to the thousandth generation, delaying retaliation for sin and wickedness....'* Just as God is called compassionate and merciful, so you should be compassionate and merciful; just as God is called righteous, so you should be righteous; just as God is called caring, so you should be caring." (Sifrei, Ekev)

Acting morally is nice, good and necessary. When embedded in a system of mitzvot, it is also holy, filling our lives with transcendent meaning. It lets us know where, or better, to Whom, we belong. A woman who started "making Pesah" only as an adult, said, in the midst of making her kitchen "kosher for Pesah,": "For the first time, I knew not only who I am, but Whose I am." What greater satisfaction can life offer?

Rambam puts it like this: "Should, however, anyone try to enforce these commandments with additional rigor... he would without doubt be foolish if he did so... he would indeed be performing improper acts, and would be unconsciously going to either one or the other extreme, thus forsaking completely the proper mean.

In this connection, I have never heard a more remarkable saying than that of the Rabbis, found in the Palestinian Talmud, in the ninth chapter of *Nedarim* (vows)... The exact words are these: Said Rabbi Iddai, in the name of Rabbi Isaac, "Do you not think that what the Law prohibits is sufficient for you that you must take upon yourself additional prohibitions?"[5]

88

Other Classical Reasons for Observing Mitzvot

Sometimes the rabbis offered more practical purposes for the system of laws.

> Rabbi Pinhas ben Yair said: [Occupying oneself with Torah] leads to prudence, prudence leads to precision, precision leads to virtuousness, virtuousness leads to modesty, modesty leads to purity, purity leads to kindliness, kindliness leads to humility, humility leads to Godfearing, Godfearing leads to holiness, holiness brings the Shekhinah, the Shekhinah leads to resurrection after death. But kindliness is greater than them all.
>
> But Rabbi Yehoshua ben Levi disagreed, for he said, humility is greater than them all." (Avodah Zara 20b)

Identifying the supreme purpose of the observance of Torah is a matter of debate even among the early rabbis. But if they disagree on the pinnacle, they all agree the ladder of holiness is ascended step by step.

Mitzvot Repair the World

If the rabbis believed that the mitzvot serve to perfect humankind, the kabbalists believed that mitzvot serve to perfect the world. In Lurianic kabbalah (which we discussed in chapter 1), God's first act in creating the world was *tzimtzum,* a withdrawing of God's self. Before creation, everything was God. There was no room for anything else. So God made room by moving over, as it were, clearing the space for the material world. But if the world were only material, with no spirit, it would be a lump, with no purpose. So after moving over, God had to re-introduce aspects of the divine into the world. To do so, God created vessels to carry the flow of divine energy from the hidden place of God to the world below.

Sadly, the material into which the divine energy flowed could not contain the divine contents. The tubes burst, and shattered into millions of shards of matter. The earthly manifestation of the flow, the Shekhinah, is trapped, in exile, in the common stuff of the world all around us. She hopes to re-unite with the Holy One, blessed be He. There is hope.

How does "occupying oneself with Torah" lead to humility?

Human beings, according to the Jewish tradition, are created in the image of God. This is a great responsibility. It is our obligation "to walk in all God's ways." How might the mitzvot, not individually, but as a system, offer individuals a means to "walk like God," or rather, to imitate God's attributes of compassion and mercy?

We might paraphrase this progression by saying: observance strengthens awareness, awareness strengthens sensitivity, sensitivity strengthens love, love strengthens acts of lovingkindness, lovingkindness strengthens one's openness to God, one's openness to God ushers one into the realm of holiness, holiness ushers God into the world.

The mitzvot are the means through which we can repair the world. With every properly done mitzvah, with every mitzvah that is performed with the right intention, we can release another spark from its material prison, and piece together the broken world. When the world is once again whole, *shaleim*, the Shekhinah (God's earthly presence) will be united with the Kudsha Brikh Hu, the Holy One, Blessed be He.

Even today, some prayerbooks instruct the reader to preface mitzvot such as putting on the tallit and tefillin by reciting the following formula:

> "For the sake of the unification of the Holy One Blessed be He, and His Shekhinah, in fear and love to unify the Name, in perfect unity, in the name of all Israel, I am ready to perform [such and such a mitzvah]... May it be your will that this commandment be considered worthy, as if I had fulfilled it in all its details, precisions, and intentions, as well as the 613 commandments that are dependent on it."

Every part of our body, every move that we make, every act we perform, when accompanied by the proper intent, can serve to repair the world, to do *tikkun olam*. Such a belief surrounds the observer with a rich atmosphere charged with the potential of God's holiness.

Building Community

Living a life of mitzvot brings us into community, one might even say communion, with our fellow Jews. The *performance* of mitzvot weaves a cloth of deeds that can join us to every other Jew. The mitzvot are our flag, our colors, that identify us as one family. Performing mitzvot gives us a piece of the corporate identity. Many Jews today keep the mitzvot out of a sense of belonging, or a desire to belong. For more than anything else, people need to belong. This sense of belonging has held many a generation of Jews together, and inspired many a Jew to observe mitzvot. For to be a Jew is to act like a Jew.☞94

Some people tell us that our acts should be grounded more firmly in beliefs; that we should contemplate, deliberate, weigh, judge and only then act. One of the most hurtful and condemnatory charges we can fling at one another is "hypocrite" - where we charge that action does not match belief. Since we believe that rituals are expressions of belief, we tend to believe that if we do not have faith, we should not observe.

Many ritual mitzvot can be done only in a certain place, only with a certain object, only at a certain time of year, only at a certain time of day. But *mitzvot bein adam l'havero* can be done anytime and anywhere, with almost anything,

These "social" mitzvot are often divided into two categories: tzedakah, those involving our money, and gemilut hesed, those involving our money, our time and our compassion.

Maimonides provides us with the classic list of the eight levels of tzedakah. They are, from highest to lowest:

8) One who strengthens the earning capacity of another by giving them a gift, or a loan, or bringing them into partnership with oneself, or finding them work so that they no longer need handouts from others.

7) One who gives to those in need without knowing to whom they are giving, and without the recipient knowing from whom they are receiving.

6) One who gives knowing whom the recipient will be while the recipient does not know who the giver is.

5) One who receives knowing from whom they are benefitting, while the giver does not know to whom they are giving.

4) One who gives without being asked.

3) One who gives after being asked.

2) One who gives less than they can but with kindness.

1) One who gives grudgingly. (Mishneh Torah, Matanot Oni'im, ch. 10)

90

Gemilut hesed is done with everything, and anything we have: our words, our acts, our gifts, our time, our kindness, our caring. No matter how much or how little money the giver has; no matter how much or little money the recipient has; we all can give - and we all can receive - acts of lovingkindness. The gemara puts It like this:

"In three ways is gemilut hesed superior to tzedakah; tzedakah is performed only with one's money, while gemilut hesed can be done with one's time or one's money. Tzedakah can only be given to the poor. Gemilut hesed can be given both to the rich and to the poor. Tzedakah can only be given to the living. Gemilut hesed can be given to the living or the dead" (Sukkot 49b)

What acts of tzedakah or hesed can you do today?

Kaplan taught that Judaism was made up of three b's: believing, belonging, and behaving. And of the three, belonging comes first.

But sociologists tell us otherwise, that our actions are determined by the group to which we belong.

"To be a human being means to be born at a particular time to a particular people, and to assume responsibility for furthering that people's civilization -- and in doing so one enhances all of human civilization. One does not need a *reason* to commit to a civilization; rather, a person finds himself or herself to be a member of a particular civilization. Civilizations are human necessities -- not luxuries...."

Theodore Weinberger, expanding on Kaplan's view, writes:

"The fact that human beings, left to themselves, inevitably create folkways and sancta [read: mitzvot] implies that to *be* human means to participate in folkways, to revere sancta."[6]

In other words, we Jews "do" mitzvot because that is what Jews do. Mitzvot have value independent of belief; they have the value of conferring identity. Therefore, we need not justify our behavior any more than we need to justify the fact that as Americans we speak English, or shake hands when we greet each other. Mitzvot are the language of the Jews.

Mitzvot Organize Our World

As linguists and psychologists tell us, language is more than a means of communication using grammar and words. Language organizes, labels, and gives value to the world around us. Living the language of mitzvot, therefore, organizes and gives value to the world around us.

Here is how one rabbinical student described her journey toward the world of mitzvot:

Returning home for Passover means confronting a choice: to eat or not to eat the non-kosher turkey at my family seder. The anticipated dilemma forces me to ask: Do I keep kosher because it is a meaningful folkway or because I sense something absolute and transcendent in my decision about what to eat?

A year ago, I would have said that I keep kosher because in doing so, I feel connected to what has long marked being a Jew...Today, I understand my keeping kosher as a way to proclaim: "I am not a

91

'person-in-general-who-happens-also-to-be-a-Jew,' but a self who is Jewish from the very essence of my soul.

But for one night, why not just eat the non-kosher turkey? Because I need to feel there is something compelling and binding about being a Jew. Because I have pushed myself to begin believing in a sense of duty to God...I am searching for what it means to live in Covenantal relationship with God.[7]

Put even more boldly, every Jew who becomes observant as a teenager or an adult does so by taking a leap of action into the world of mitzvot, even as our ancestors did at the foot of Mt. Sinai when they responded to the revelation of God saying - *All that God has said,* **na'aseh v'nishma,** *we will do and we will listen.* (Shemot 24:7) We can read and study and imagine what mitzvot are all about; and how it feels to observe. But, sooner or later, we just have to jump in. Mitzvot lose something in the translation. For it is in the doing that we gain understanding. As we enter the world of mitzvot, the world of mitzvot enters us.☞94

☞94

Mitzvot, like all rituals and acts, are not just expressions or enactments of beliefs. They are also the creators, reinforcers and carriers of belief. In Heschel's words, a Jew is asked "to do more than he understands in order to understand more than he does. In carrying out the word of the Torah, he is ushered into the presence of the spiritual meaning."[8]

We become what we do, so we must be careful about what we do.

What do you think is meant by "leap of action?"

How do our actions affect who we are?

EXERCISE 1: Loving the Law

The first paragraph of the Sh'ma is one of the central prayer passages discussing our love for God. In that paragraph, a connection is made between love and law. God demonstrates God's love for the Jewish people by giving the law, and the Jewish people demonstrate their love by observing the law.

Describe how giving or observing the law might be indicative of love. Consider the statement made by many parents when disciplining their children - "This hurts me more than it hurts you." Are there parallels to rules created by governments for their citizens?

_____

_____

_____

_____

_____

_____

EXERCISE 2: Three Dimensional Halakhah

View the "MAGIC EYE" picture on page 119. [Turn this book to the right to view accurately.] On page 120 you will find a small picture showing the 3D image you will see when you find and train your MAGIC EYE.

> "Hold the image so that it touches your nose. Let the eyes relax, and stare vacantly off into space, as if looking through the image. Relax and become comfortable with the idea of observing the image, without looking at it. When you are relaxed and not crossing your eyes, move the page slowly away from your face. Perhaps an inch every two or three seconds. Keep looking through the page. Stop at a comfortable reading distance and keep staring. The most discipline is needed when something starts to 'come in,' because at that moment you'll instinctively try to look at the page rather than looking through it. If you look at it, start again."[9]

How does this help us to better understand halakhah?

EXERCISE 3: Lessons of Mitzvot

List five mitzvot and describe the lessons you think they come to teach us.

_____

_____

_____

_____

_____

_____

_____

EXERCISE 4: Moments of Meeting

List five symbols and sites for meeting godliness. Be creative.

_____

_____

_____

_____

_____

_____

EXERCISE 5: Judaism's Corporate Identity

Explain what it means that a company has a "corporate identity?" Give some examples that you are familiar with. How would you describe Judaism's corporate identity and describe the place of mitzvot in that process? After answering these questions, create a commercial which will exemplify Judaism's corporate identity.

_____

_____

_____

_____

_____

_____

_____

EXERCISE 6: Doing vs. Comprehending

Imagine that a Jewish friend tells you that he wants to become more Jewishly observant. Do you tell him that he should first understand what he is doing before he becomes more observant or do you tell him to "jump-in" to the rituals and he can learn about them along the way. Would your answer be different than the traditional Jewish answer? Why?

_____

_____

_____

Chapter 7:
Sacred Space

The Jewish people was born when Abraham was called to journey to a promised land.

> *"Go from your homeland, your place of birth, your father's house,"* God called to Abraham, *"to the land that I will show you."* (Bereshit 12:1)

With these words, God began a very special relationship with the Jewish people. In every generation, in every human soul, this call is renewed, for the spiritual enterprise is a journey from a "place" where we begin to seek God to a "place" where we believe we can find God. It is a journey first undertaken by a people who recorded it and mapped it and preserved it for their children. And it is a journey undertaken by their children, who must learn to walk the journey on their own.

Holiness Flows from the Land

Sometimes, we may set out on a very ordinary journey unaware of how amazing it will become. This is what happened to Jacob, our father. When he left home, fleeing his brother, he found God. Or, rather, God found him.

> *And Jacob stopped at a place and stayed there for the night...and behold, God stood over him and said, I am the Lord, the God of Abraham your grandfather, and Isaac. This land that you lie on, I will give to you and your children." Jacob awoke from his sleep and said, truly God is in this place, and I did not know it... This is a gateway to heaven.* (Bereshit 28:15)

Jacob lay down, tired and unaware, that holiness was flowing from the land he was on. Sacred space in Judaism is the place where Jews and God meet each other. For the first two thousand years, Israel was that sacred space. For two thousand years, God chose the place:

> *The land where you are going is not like the land of Egypt... rather the land that you are going to possess is ... a land which God cares for. The eyes of God are always upon it, from the beginning of the year until the very end.* (Devarim 11:11-12)

The Torah ends with the Jews on the east bank of the River Jordan, just short of Israel, as if to say, the Torah is the never-ending story.

Have you sensed God's presence at a time when you least expected it?

96

And after choosing the land of Israel, God chose its capital:

> *Upon dedicating the Temple that he had built, King Solomon said: Blessed is the Lord God of Israel, who made a promise to my father David and fulfilled it. For He said, From the time I brought My people out of the land of Egypt, I never chose a city from among all the tribes of Israel to build my house where my Name might abide... but then I chose Jerusalem for my name to abide there....* (II Divrei HaYamim 6:1-4)

So the land became our destination and, ultimately, our home designated so by God and the generations of Jews who lived and died there. It was the only place we wanted to be, and the only place where we could be fully Jewish. To be away from Israel was exile. To be home again was glorious.

> *When the Lord brought back those who returned to Zion, we were as dreamers. Our mouths were filled with laughter and our tongues with joy....* (Tehillim 126:1-2)

> *I rejoiced when they told me, we are going to Jerusalem. And now our feet are standing in your gates....* (Tehillim 122:1)

While **Ramban** lived a thousand years after the destruction of the Temple, he captured the passion that Jews thousands of years earlier felt for their land:

> The beauty of the world is the Land of Israel.
>
> The beauty of the Land of Israel is Jerusalem.
>
> The beauty of Jerusalem is the Sanctuary.
>
> The beauty of the Sanctuary is the site of the Holy of Holies.
>
> The beauty of the Holy of Holies is the place of the cherubim,
>
> for the Divine Glory resides there,
>
> as it is said,
>
> "And there will I meet with thee
> and I will speak with thee from above the ark-cover,
> from between the two cherubim."[1] (Shemot 25:22)

Yehuda Halevi wrote of the pain of exile: "My heart is in the east, but I am in the furthermost west. How can I find pleasure in food? How can it be sweet for me? How can I render my vows and bonds when Zion lies enslaved?"

Tehillim 126 is the Shir HaMaalot prayer which precedes Birkat HaMazon (the Grace after meals) on Shabbat and holidays. Why do you think that this selection was chosen to be recited at that time?

Ramban (1194-1270), also known as Rabbi Moses ben Nahman, or Nahmonides, lived in Spain most of his life. A leading Torah commentator and talmud scholar, he emigrated to Israel, where he lived the last three years of his life.

Israel was the place that drew our affection and our imagination. It held our hearts and our souls. We were intimate with the land of Israel. We gave her our love. She offered us her comfort and shelter. She was a manifestation of God; we became one with her.

> They that trust in the Lord are as Mount Zion, which cannot be moved, but abides forever. As the mountains are around Jerusalem, so the Lord is around his people from this time forth and forever more. (Tehillim 125:1-2)

The rabbis spoke of her just as intimately:

> Ulla who had come to Babylonia from the land of Israel, became ill and was about to die. His friends reassured him that they would bury him in Israel. He responded, And what benefit is that to me? ... Losing one's soul in the lap of a strange women cannot be compared to surrendering it in the lap of one's mother. (Yerushalmi Kilayim 9:4)

Inside the boundaries of Israel, the land was holy. The space, the towns, and the very soil itself. The land could not tolerate sin, or immorality, or wrongdoing. If the Jews turned away from God, the Torah tells us, the land would spit them out, and refuse to give forth fruit. God would, as it were, no longer choose to meet the Jewish people there if the Jews no longer chose to meet God. There could be no sacred space where there is no sacred meeting.

The Temple

If sacred space is where God and Israel choose to meet, then the holiest place in the biblical world was the Temple. It was seen as the place where God's presence flowed into the world, as it were, and the place where the Jews went to greet God.

For the pious Jew of the biblical period, physical proximity to the Temple equaled spiritual proximity to God:

> "One thing I ask of the Lord, only that do I seek: to live in the house of the Lord all the days of my life, to gaze upon the beauty of the Lord, to frequent His Temple." (Tehillim 27:4)

To be far from God physically was to be far from God spiritually.

What does it mean that "we were intimate with the land of Israel?"

"The air of your Land, is the very life of our soul."
Yehuda Halevi

It is true that all the world is holy, for all the world is the work of God: "Holy, holy, holy is the Lord of hosts, the fullness of the earth is His glory" (Isaiah 6:3); "The heavens are Yours and the earth too, You founded the world and all that is in it" (Tehillim 89:12). Yet, the rabbis taught that there are different degrees of holiness in the world. The world, as it were, possesses concentric circles of holiness. All the world is holy, but the land of Israel is holier than other lands. All the cities in Israel are holy, but Jerusalem is holier than all the other cities. All the places in Jerusalem are holy, but the Temple is holier than her other places. All the Temple is holy, but the Holy of Holies the holiest place of all.

98

Do we have a concept of sacred space today? How would you define it? Where do you find it?

"Why, O Lord, do you stand aloof, heedless in times of trouble?" (Tehillim 10:1)

"You, O Lord, be not far off, my Strength, hasten to my aid." (Tehillim 22:20)

While in Israel, Jews were in the *daled amot,* the living-room, of God. Living in Israel gave the Jews purpose, security and abiding worth.

Come, let us go up to the mountain of the Lord, to the house of the God of Jacob; that he may teach us his ways and that we may walk in his paths, for out of Zion shall go forth the law and the word of the Lord from Jerusalem. (Isaiah 2:1-4)

And, as the rabbis taught, living in Israel gave them extraordinary rewards:

The sins of the one who lives in Palestine are forgiven, as it is written, And the inhabitants shall not say, I am sick; the people that dwell in the land shall be forgiven their iniquity. (Isaiah 33:24)

To be outside of Israel, then, was not just to be far from one's homeland, or far from one's family. It was to be far from God, far from God's teachings and far from the power of salvation.

From the days of the first exile in 586 BCE, Jews far from Israel tried to close the distance by sending contributions to the Temple; and by facing Jerusalem in their prayers.

When Israel was again conquered in the year 70 C.E., the Second Temple was destroyed. Nearly seventy years later, the Bar Kochba rebellion, designed to liberate Jerusalem, was squashed. We were left without a Temple, and without hope that it would be rebuilt soon. We were left without a place for God's name to abide, without a place to go in times of loss, joy or need, and without a place to direct our prayers.

But the rabbis responded with a most creative vision. Out of the texts, practices and imagination of the Jewish people, they crafted a portable world of the Temple and the land of Israel. Houses of Study became surrogates for the Temple, prayers surrogates for sacrifices, and rabbis - and, potentially, all Jews - surrogates for the priests. The Temple and its allure, and our hopes for its restoration, were preserved in our prayers and songs:

> *"Bring us safely from the four corners of the earth, and restore us, upright and proud, to our land."* (Shacharit [morning] service)

> *"Return in kindness to your city Jerusalem, and dwell there as you have promised..."* (weekday amidah)

Through this creative transference, the holiness of the Temple and the Land of Israel soared above political, and geographic boundaries, and traveled with the Jews into exile.

If we could no longer flourish in the land, the land would flourish in us. As the **Baal Shem Tov** taught: "Wherever a person is in his thoughts, there he is indeed. Therefore, if a person lives outside of the Land of Israel, but thinks about Israel constantly, it is as if he were there."[2]

This was the magic of cyberspace before its time. All prayers, places and worshippers were united in a network of holiness, connected instantaneously through time and beyond space. All prayers were directed toward Jerusalem; all eyes and hearts turned toward Jerusalem; and from Jerusalem holiness was beamed back around the world. At the end of every seder and the end of every Yom Kippur, no matter where in the world we are, we recite as one: Next year in Jerusalem. And for that one moment of hope and prayer, we are all there. ☞104

Embassies of Holiness

> "When the Temple was destroyed, the Holy One blessed be He scattered the stones all over the world. And on every place where a stone fell, a synagogue would be erected. Therefore, each synagogue is called "a little Temple" (mikdash me'at) because it contains a little of the Temple."[3]

The land's holiness was no longer bound in place and soil. It was released and transformed into a pulsing stream of holiness which could flow to Jewish settlements throughout the world. Rav Kook, the first Chief Rabbi of the land of Israel in the 20th century wrote:

> "Israel is the spatial center of holiness in the world, radiating holiness vertically to the Jews who live upon the land as well as horizontally to other portions and peoples of the earth"[4] ☞104

The **Baal Shem Tov** was the founder of Hasidism. Central to his teachings were love and concern for the uneducated, simple Jew, as well as emphasizing the absolute joy of divine worship.

Those who are in Jerusalem say: "Next year in Jerusalem re-built."

The Ropshitzer Rebbe taught that it is only through all of our efforts combined that Jerusalem can be rebuilt: "By our service to God we build Jerusalem daily. One of us adds a row, another only a brick. When Jerusalem is completed, Redemption will come."

100

Hallah is the name of the bread-stuffs given as an offering to the priests. Salt was used in all the sacrifices.

What are the benefits and potential dangers of the Jews choosing the places to meet God?

While Israel and Jerusalem remain the capital of holiness, our synagogues, houses of study, homes and moments of mitzvah are all embassies of holiness. In them we discover and recreate the holiness that hovered above the Holy of Holies in the Temple, and meet the Shekhinah, God's named presence on earth.

In the synagogue, the *shaliah tzibbur*, the one who leads the congregation in prayer, stands in place of the High Priest and recites the Priestly Blessing during the repetition of the amidah:

> *May the Lord bless you and keep you.*
>
> *May the Lord shine his countenance upon you and be gracious unto you.*
>
> *May the Lord show you kindness and grant you peace.*

Our prayers are substitutes for the sacrifices.

In the home, the dining room table is transformed into the altar. We approach it with ritual cleanliness. Therefore, we wash our hands before eating bread and use salt on our **hallah**.

There is an old Yiddish prayer which women once recited before Shabbat candlelighting that transformed them into the High Priest and their home into the Temple:

> "Lord of the World, may my mitzvah of kindling the lights be accepted like the mitzvah of the high priest who kindled the lights in the dear Temple. 'Your word is a lamp to my feet, a light to my path.' May the feet of my children walk on God's path, and may the mitzvah of my candlelighting be acceptable so that my children's eyes may be enlightened in the dear Torah. Dear God, accept my mitzvah of the lights as if my candles were the olive oil lamps which burned in the Temple and were never extinguished."

Through such acts, both actor and place are exalted and God and Jew meet. In the time of the Bible, God chose the place to meet the Jews and the Jews came. After the destruction, the Jews choose the places to meet God, and God comes.

Every Place Can Be Sacred Space

God comes into the daily and weekly lives of Jews around the world.

101

Rabbi Shimon bar Yohai taught, Come and see how precious are the Jews in the eyes of the Holy One blessed be He, for wherever the Jews go in the world, the Shekhinah goes with them. (Megillah 29a)

The rabbis codified this sense of presence through the formula they crafted for the various blessings that we say hundreds of times every day: *"Barukh ata..."* "Blessed are You, God..." You, the One who stands before us, the One who stands with us, the One whom we can turn to and feel present in our lives.

The Lurianic kabbalists invigorate our sense of the holiness in the everywhere through their belief in the *kelipot,* the shards of the primordial vessels that broke under the strain of carrying the flow of the divine into the physical world. Each object we touch possesses a spark of the divine. It is our task to recognize it and free it so it can rejoin with its source.

Indeed, we make holy space in every Jewish home through the elegant ritual of attaching a mezuzah. As the words of the mezuzah remind us, we do not need the Temple or sacrifices or any public, formal space to feel God's presence. We can feel God's presence, we should feel God's presence, when we rise up or when we lie down, when we help a friend, visit the sick, give a gift to the needy, or show kindness to a stranger. All we need to do is be aware of the godliness of our acts, and the presence of the Shekhinah.

Rabbi Levi Yitzhak of Berditchev put this sense of God's constant presence this way: (Dudele song)

Where I wander - You;
Where I ponder - You
Only you, you again,
Always you.

You! You! You!

When I am gladdened You;
When I am saddened You;
Only You, You again,
Always You.

You! You! You!

Sky is You, Earth is You;
You above, You below;
In every trend, at every end,
Only You, You again
Always You.

You! You! You![5]

102

Mizrach means east, and the art is so called because it is placed on the eastern wall.

In all ways, through mitzvot, prayers, synagogues, schools, homes, work, playgrounds and ballfields, for two thousand years, we have turned our place in the world into God's place. Yet we never forgot to turn toward God's place, Jerusalem. The arks in our synagogues point the way toward Jerusalem; when we stand in prayer our feet point us toward Jerusalem; adorning our walls at home is a piece of art, called a *mizrah*, pointing the way toward Jerusalem.

For two thousand years of exile we learned how to live well and fully in holiness's embassies around the world, for the capital of holiness was not ours.

And then, in 1948, and more fully in 1967, the capital of holiness became ours once again. Heschel noted that, about the return of Jews to the State of Israel, and the return of the State of Israel to the Jews: "We have not even begun to fathom the meaning of this great event."[6]

Today, more than any other time in Jewish history, we have both a vibrant Israel and a dynamic diaspora; the source and the outposts; the capital and the embassies. We are learning how to choose to live in one without diminishing the other. We learned over 2000 years how to bring the source of holiness to our places throughout the world. And we will continue to do this.☞105

But the land of Israel still possesses a unique majesty and mystery. It continues to yield universal lessons of holiness, even as it did in days past. The victory of its independence, so soon after the Holocaust, offered hope to the world at a time of terrible darkness. The return to our homeland served, in Heschel's mind, to restore the hope of redemption to an otherwise damned world:

> "The State of Israel is not the fulfillment of the Messianic promise, but it makes the Messianic promise plausible... All of us [Jew and non-Jew] must learn how to create in this dreadful emptiness of our lives, how to be illumined by a hope despite disaster and dismay."

In Elie Wiesel's mind, the restoration of Jerusalem to the people Israel served to bring the promise of homecoming to all those who perished so far from their mother's lap.

"Immediately upon hearing that the Old City had been liberated, Elie Wiesel began to run to the Wall. When he reached it, breathless, he was approached by an elderly Jew ... [who] remarked to him: "Do

you know why and how we defeated the enemy and liberated Jerusalem? Because six million souls took part in the battle." Then I actually saw what the naked eye seldom sees: souls on fire floated high above us, praying to the Creator to protect them and all of us. And this prayer itself was also transformed into a soul."[7]

Even as our relationship with God has changed, so has our relationship with the Land of Israel. Even as the land hallows us, our return has hallowed the land. And even as we liberate our holy space, our holy space liberates us.

For two thousand years we thought of ourselves as a religion of time, with Shabbat our cathedral, as Heschel called it. The State of Israel has returned us to a religion of space. The significance of this development is still unfolding.

104

EXERCISE 1: Cyberspace of Holiness

Explain what you think the author meant when she stated "this was cyberspace before its time." Do you think this is a useful metaphor? Why or why not?

_____

_____

_____

_____

_____

EXERCISE 2: Israel at the Center

Write a letter to the Prime Minister of Israel addressing the following questions. Is Israel fulfilling Rav Kook's dream of serving as a source of holiness to the world? How could it do better? Be specific.

_____

_____

_____

_____

_____

_____

_____

EXERCISE 3: Israel and the Diaspora

Since living in Israel is a real possibility for us today, is it sufficient to create embassies of sacred space outside of Israel? Why or why not? How would you react to someone who stated that all Jews should make aliyah. (Making aliyah - literally "going up" - refers to moving to Israel.)

_____

_____

_____

_____

_____

_____

_____

_____

Chapter 8:
Building a Life of Holiness Day by Day

Weaving Every Moment

Heschel once wrote that we should live our lives as if they were works of art. Every act is like a brush stroke and every thought a color. Together, and over time, we create out of our deeds the masterpiece of our lives.

I like to imagine that my masterpiece as a cloth, endlessly woven from my moves, my words, my intents, and my attitudes. As such, my fabric holds the record of my daily kindnesses and painful mistakes. It reveals the times I have pulled the threads too tightly, closing myself off to those around me, and the times I have been too lax and loose, threatening the fabric's integrity, and mine. My cloth has woven into it the faces and gifts and hurts and joys of the thousands of people who have touched my life. It is honest, sometimes brutal. But mostly, it inspires me, for I know that everything I do leaves a legacy for good or bad, far beyond my original intentions. When a butterfly beats its wings in China, we are told, the winds stir over America.

And unlike a piece of art that hangs on a wall, this is art that I can gather up and spread over the pain and loneliness and grief of others, offering comfort, shelter and warmth. It can be used as a shield against the cold. We can dance with it in celebration, hide or strut or rest in it. It is the tallit of my deeds that embraces me even after I die.

Each of us can imagine a different medium and look for our own artwork. It can be of wood or stone, on canvas or felt, clay or metal, or of materials found only in the imagination. But we should take the time to imagine it, and consider how we build it day by day, deed by deed.

To see our lives as art is to know that there is no such thing as an inconsequential act. How we treat the cashier at the store, how we act toward those we don't like, how we conduct ourselves when no one else is around, all these things leave a legacy in the weave of our fabric.☞112

What is your favorite piece of clothing? Why do you like it? What about the fabric is attractive to you? If you own a tallit which you purchased, why did you choose to buy that particular one?

What kind of masterpiece are you building with your life?

"Parashat T'tzaveh, in Shemot, provides a glimpse into the glorification of the minute, tiny, and seemingly insignificant. The building of the mishkan (tabernacle) is described, and while the task is assigned to Betzalel and Oholiav, every Israelite had a job, even if it only meant carrying wood from here to there. Only the leaders of the enterprise have their names memorialized in the Torah, but the effort of every individual in the community was needed to complete the task. This teaches us that the very humblest of tasks is required to complete an endeavor. So too is a life. A life is not made up only of the broad strokes of birth, profession, family and death. It is made up of the choices we make each day. Each daily act builds our own mishkan, wherein God may dwell." - D.C.

108

Rabbi Leib, son of Sarah, the hidden tzaddik who wandered around the world said:

"I did not go to the Maggid (a great hasidic rebbe) to hear Torah from him. I went to see how he untied his laces and tied them up again."[1]

Torah is not just what we find in texts, or what we speak or study. It is also the way we choose to conduct the affairs of our lives. Believing that every moment is significant, that every act has the potential to unlock a bit of holiness hidden in the world, unites our discrete acts of study, prayer, mitzvot, and kindliness into a seamless thread of holiness. And it is with this thread that we weave our *moments* of holiness into *a life* of holiness.

Too often we lurch from one spiritual "moment" to another. But Judaism is about more than just giving us moments of holiness. It is about giving us a life of holiness.

Daniel Matt puts it this way:

> "Our spiritual task is to discover the divine sparks in each person and situation we encounter, to become aware that every single thing that we do, see, touch, or imagine... [has the possibility of being laden with holiness.] Raising the sparks is a powerful metaphor. It transforms religion from a list of do's and don'ts, or a list of dogmas, into a spiritual adventure."[2]

Judaism is about *acting* in the *world*. It is about reaching out and making a difference. Many think that spirituality begins with a journey inward, seeking the truth inside us. Judaism believes that spirituality begins with a journey outward (remember Abraham and Sarah, "Go from the land of your birth...."), seeking the holiness all around us.

Reaching outward also means reaching forward - toward each other, the world, and godliness. Judaism is not meant to be a lonely task. It is not something we can seek to do alone. It is something we do together. The Torah tells us this, the rabbis tell us this, and, most recently, sociologists tell us this.

"Man cannot be conceived of apart from the continuous outpouring of himself into the world... Human being [or being human] cannot be understood as somehow resting within itself, in some closed sphere of interiority, and then setting out to express itself... Human being *is* externalizing in its essence...."[4]

"Franz Rosenzweig once suggested that some day, as religious insight broadened, a mother's recipe for gefilte fish would be passed on in the family, bearing with it the same sense of tradition as do formal commandments or customs. Every act of social justice, every humane or productive factory, every sport contest in community centers, every act of human socializing and dignity will become a secularized halakhah as Jewish religious insight deepens and the sacred dimensions of the profane are uncovered."[4]

"The Jew does not stand alone before God; it is as a member of the community that he stands before God. Our relationship to Him is not as an I to a Thou but a we to a Thou."[5]

Becoming Through Doing

Humans don't so much "become" and then "do" as we first "do" and in the process "become." We cannot become a teacher until we teach. We cannot become an athlete until we play. Judaism knows that often, our attitudes are built by our actions, just as much as our actions can be built by our attitudes.

We are also learning that when we cause our bodies to relax, our minds begin to relax. We are learning that when we force ourselves to smile, we can begin to feel happier. When we dress up, we stand taller. So it is with holiness. We gain a sense of God and godliness by acting godly. Just as we said regarding prayer, that sometimes the act of prayer comes before the impulse to pray, so here too the act of holiness sometimes comes before the feeling of holiness. Too often we feel we have to wait for the right mood, or the right moment; that we can't force these things; that if our inside doesn't match our outside, we aren't being honest.

Judaism knows that by doing we can create the mood; by acting holy we can become holy. After all, it is ever so much easier to control our actions than to control our feelings.

Judaism teaches us what to do, so we can become God's partners in life. For that is our task in life: to tend to the world and finish what God began at creation. A popular musar (ethical) saying is: "Never ask if something is possible. Ask if it is necessary. If it is, and there is no path, then blaze a path."[5]

There are so many things that need doing, so many paths that we must travel and blaze. Some paths may be bigger than others; some may bring more prestige than others. But, if we believe that holiness can be released in every task we do, depending on how we do it, then we need not lament that right now we are walking on this path, and not that one. We can affect the world here and now, right where we are. In a little while, we can change paths.

"Soon after the death of Rabbi Moshe, Rabbi Mendl of Kotzk asked one of his disciples: "What was most important to your teacher?"

The disciple thought and then replied: "Whatever he happened to be doing at the moment."[6]

Rabbi Lawrence Kushner asks that we imagine that each person is like an incomplete jigsaw puzzle. Everyone's pieces have gotten

"There is a great comfort in finding ourselves part of a greater whole. We are not lost. We matter as part of our community. Each of us is needed, and God values us as part of God's chosen people.

But sometimes we want to feel that in times of pain or confusion that God is taking notice of us as individuals. At times like this, while we take comfort in our membership in Israel, we can also look to the siddur for reminders that God does pay attention to each of us. From Tehillim 31 a verse has found its way into the weekday ma'ariv (evening) service and in a slightly changed version, into Adon Olam: "b'yadkha afkid ruḥi - into Your hand I commit my spirit." In the weekday shacharit (morning) service and the Shabbat minḥa (afternoon) service we read: "My spirit, which is on you and the words that you speak because I have placed them there - My presence and My lessons shall not depart from you, from your children, or your children's children, says God, from now until forever.

The next time you pray, remember two things. Remember that you are speaking to God in ancient words, together with Jews all over the world. You are bound to all these different kinds of Jews by the words you say and the times you say them. But at the same time, God's spirit is on you. You. You have the choice to place your soul into God's care. You are significant as part of the eternal people. You are also significant as the unique you that God has created." - D.C.

110

mixed up. I have pieces that belong to you, and you have pieces that belong to me. Neither of us can become complete without receiving pieces from another. And neither of us can feel finished until we give our extra pieces away.

And such exchanges happen more often than we think, without our even knowing it. In a chance conversation or a casual act of kindness, we may offer up a piece that completes the other's puzzle. Or when we turn away from a moment's encounter, we may realize that we are a little more complete than we were before.

Sharing the Burden

One of life's most satisfying feelings comes from knowing we have helped someone else. *Pirkei Avot* 6:6 teaches us that one of the most important things we can do in life is share one another's burden. True, each of us is an individual, and has to shoulder the bulk of our own burdens. No one can relieve us of this fate. But, being alone does not mean we have to be lonely. Judaism teaches that we must be there for each other; be there with each other. And this is something we can do every day.

The Torah teaches us this in its very first chapters. Eve was created in response to Adam's loneliness. *"It is not good for the human to be alone,"* God realized. *"I will make for him an ezer kenegdo, a worthy helper"* to stand beside him. She will fill the void, shielding Adam from the loneliness beyond.

Eve was created to stand before Adam, to fill his emptiness.

But this raises a question. If God was there, why did Adam feel alone? And why did God not respond to Adam's loneliness by saying, *hineni,* here I am?

Because God did not, could not, fill the void of human loneliness. For God was commander and the human was commanded. God was all powerful and the human was not. God was Creator and the human the created.

The distance was too great. Comfort needs to come from someone close and physical, someone who is warm and who puts their arms around you, and someone who shares the experience of vulnerability. Since God could not be physically present for Adam, God created an *ezer*, a worthy helper, *kenegdo*, to be a surrogate of God.

Everyone needs a central text around which to fashion the story of their lives. The text will certainly change over time, as we grow and change. We may even spend more of our lives searching for the text than actually having one. But not to worry: the search then becomes the text of our lives. The text is the thread that we use to weave together the disparate experiences we have. For now, I have chosen this story of being an *ezer* - a surrogate for God - as my text, my thread. You too, now, can seek a text for yourself.

111

Adam and Eve are models for all people. At times, each of us is Adam, lonely and in need; at times, each of us is Eve, God's surrogate. But to be God's surrogate is no easy task. So Judaism teaches us how, each and every day. When we respond to the burdens of another, when we stand before others to shield them from the loneliness, we become not only more human. We become more divine.

In Judaism, spirituality can be found in the actions of the everyday. The capacity to do good can be turned into acts of holiness. And when our acts are infused with holiness, so are we.☞112

You have now reached the end of this book. Soon, you will close it and look up. You will see another person's face; hear another's person voice. You will have a choice of what to do, or at least how to do it. Remember that whatever you do, you are encountering a surragate of God; and you can respond as a surrogate of God. Now, go and do, and build your masterpiece.

Who do you go to when you seek comfort? What do they do that comforts you? Do you think that you bring comfort to others?

EXERCISE 1: The Masterpiece of Our Life

"Each of us can imagine a different medium and look for our own artwork. It can be of wood or stone, on canvas or felt, clay or metal, or of materials found only in the imagination. But we should take the time to imagine it, and consider how we build it day by day, deed by deed."

Describe or illustrate the masterpiece of your life.

EXERCISE 2: Becoming God's Partner

List all of the things that you do everyday that make you more divine. And think of all the things you can do tomorrow that make you God's ezer.

_____

_____

_____

_____

_____

We are Not Alone

Rabbi Lawrence Kushner has drawn something which reminds us that we are not alone; that the holiness we release into the world becomes holiness that flows to others. He calls his drawing "The Loving Star" and it came about like this:

"Since Levy's birth, six months ago, everyone's position in the family has obviously undergone profound change. We have all had to do some adjusting as a new soul began to take his place in our family system. The children especially were worried whether or not there would still be enough love to go around and took to quarrelling even more than usual. And then I came up with this idea.

On a piece of paper with everyone watching on, I drew a figure that looked something like this:

There was much excitement. 'Daddy, what is it?' But, I just went on drawing. Then in each circle I wrote the name of one of our family. Then I drew arrows, pointed in both directions extending between each person and everyone else in the family. I explained to everyone that the arrows were lines of loving and that the more love someone 'put out' into the system - since every channel flowed in two directions but also sooner or later led back to itself - the more one 'got back.' I wrote at the top, 'The loving always comes back to you' and at the bottom 'You can't take loving, you can only give loving.' And I titled it, 'The Kushner Family Loving Star.' We taped it to the wall at a young one's eye level.

Every now and then I notice that one of the children is quietly studying the star. They trace the lines with their finger. Somehow drawing some reassurance from the drawing's truth."[7]

Make the design above into your Loving Star. Write your name in one of the circles. Fill in the other circles too. Keep this beside your bed, and be sure to look at it everyday. It will remind you where you are, who you are, and perhaps most important, Whose you are.

And with that knowledge, may all your days be filled with holiness, and all your nights with peace.

Endnotes

Chapter 1

1. "הכניסיני תחת כנפך" - אהבת חן : שירי אהבה

2. Translation from <u>The Five Books of Moses (The Schocken Bible, Volume 1)</u>,New York:Schocken, 1995, by Everett Fox.

3. Translation from <u>Machzor for Rosh Hashanah and Yom Kippur</u>, New York:Rabbinical Assembly, 1975, edited by Rabbi Jules Harlow.

4 - 5. Translation from <u>Siddur Sim Shalom</u>, New York:Rabbinical Assembly and United Synagogue of Conservative Judaism, 1985, edited by Rabbi Jules Harlow, Page 19.

6. Translation from <u>The Teachings of Maimonides</u>, New Jersey:Jason Aronson, 1992, by Jacob Minkin, page 160.

7. Martin Buber, <u>Tales of the Hasidim: Early Masters</u>, New York:Schocken, 1991, page 269.

8. By Daniel C. Matt, from <u>God & the Big Bang: Discovering Harmony Between Science & Spirituality</u>, copyright Daniel C. Matt. Woodstock, VT:Jewish Lights Publishing, 1996, pages 80 - 81. $21.95 hc + $3.50 s/h. Order by mail or call 800-962-4544. Permission granted by Jewish Lights Publishing, P.O. Box 237, Woodstock, VT 05091.

9. Mordecai M. Kaplan, <u>The Meaning Of God in Modern Jewish Religion</u>, 1937 & 1962, page 27 - 28.

10. <u>The Meaning Of God</u> by Mordechai Kaplan, page 26.

11. <u>The Meaning Of God</u> by Mordechai Kaplan, page 30.

12. Abraham Joshua Heschel, <u>God in Search of Man</u>, New York:Farrar, Straus, and Giroux, 1955, page 7.

13. Abraham Joshua Heschel, <u>God in Search of Man</u>, page 21.

14. Yochanan Muffs, <u>Love and Joy: Law, Language and Religion in Ancient Israel</u>, Belknap Press, 1995.

15. Adapted from <u>Higher and Higher: Making Jewish Prayer Part of Us</u>, by Steven M. Brown; New York:United Synagogue Youth, 1980, page 65.

16. Adapted from <u>Higher and Higher</u> by Steven Brown, page 66.

17. Adapted from <u>Higher and Higher</u> by Steven Brown, page 62.

Chapter 2

1. Sh'ma: Journal of Jewish Responsibility, 27/522.

2. <u>Jewish Spirituality: From the Bible Through the Middle Ages, vol. 1</u>, Arthur Green, ed., Crossroad Publishing Co.,1989, page xiii.

3. "A Journey in Seven Stages" in <u>Jewish Spiritual Journeys: 20 Essays Written to Honor the Occassion of the 70th Birthday of Eugene Borowitz</u>, Lawrence Hoffman and Arnold Wolf, eds., Behrman House, 1997, page 159.

4 As told by Rabbi Ismar Schorsch at the 1996 Rabbinical Assembly Convention.

5. Abraham Joshua Heschel, <u>Man's Quest for God</u>, MacMillan Publishing Co., 1954 & 1981, page 88.

6. Yitzhak Buxbaum, <u>Jewish Spiritual Practices</u>, New Jersey:Jason Aronson, 1994.

7. Martin Buber, <u>Tales of the Hasidim: Early Masters</u>, page 193.

8. Martin Buber, <u>Tales of the Hasidim: Early Masters</u>, page 56.

9. <u>Jewish Spirituality: From the Bible Through the Middle Ages, vol. 2</u>, Arthur Green, ed., Crossroad Publishing Co.,1989, page 219.

10. <u>Mesillat Yesharim: Path of the Just</u>, New Jersey:Jason Aronson, page 450.

11. Heschel, <u>Man's Quest for God</u>, page 133.

Chapter 3

1. Sh'ma: Journal of Jewish Responsibility, 24/475.

2. David Weiss Halivni, <u>The Book and the Sword</u>, Farrar, Straus, & Giroux,1996.

Chapter 4

1. Byron Sherwin, <u>Sparks Amidst the Ashes</u>, Oxford Press, 1997, page 101.

2. Matt, <u>God & the Big Bang</u>, page 105.

3. Heschel, <u>Man's Quest for God</u>, page 8.

4 Abraham Joshua Heschel, <u>The Insecurity of Freedom</u>, New York:Schocken, 1985.

5. Sh'ma: A Journal of Jewish Responsibility, 27/516.

6. Sherwin, <u>Sparks Amidst the Ashes</u>, page 118.

7. Sherwin, <u>Sparks Amidst the Ashes</u>, page 117.

8. Diagram from: Steven Brown, <u>Reclaiming Our Legacy</u>, New York:USY, 1986, pages 268 - 269.

Chapter 5

1. Heschel, <u>Man's Quest for God</u>, page 87.

2. Heschel, <u>Man's Quest for God</u>, page 5.

3. L'kutei Yekarim 10a as quoted in <u>Your Word is Fire</u>, eds.Arthur Green and Barry Holtz,

4 Naomi Rachel Remens, <u>Kitchen Table Wisdom</u>, Riverhead Books, 1996.

5. Bahya ibn Pekuda, et al., <u>Duties of the Heart</u>, New Jersey:Jason Aronson, 1996.

6. Eliezer Berkovitz, <u>Studies in Torah Judaism: Prayer No. 5</u>, New York:Yeshiva U, 1962.

7. Kaplan, <u>The Meaning of God</u>, page 33

8. Likutei Etzot Ha-Shem as quoted in <u>A Treasury of Thoughts in Jewish Prayer</u>, ed. Sidney Greenberg, New Jersey:Jason Aronson, 1996.

9. Kathleen Norris, "Why the Psalms Scare Us," <u>Christianity Today</u>, July 15, 1996, page 20.

10. Heschel, <u>Man's Quest for God</u>, page 97.

11. Heschel, <u>Man's Quest for God</u>, page 37.

12. <u>Out of the Depths I Call to You: A Book of Prayers for the Married Jewish Woman</u>, ed. Nina Beth Cardin, New Jersey:Jason Aronson, 1995.

13. Norris, <u>Christianity Today</u>.

14. Ferdinand M. Isserman Sermons and Addresses as quoted in <u>A Treasury of Thoughts in Jewish Prayer</u>, ed. Sidney Greenberg, New Jersey:Jason Aronson, 1996, page 22.

15. Heschel, <u>Man's Quest for God</u>, page 31.

16. Buxbaum, <u>Jewish Spiritual Practices</u>, page 102.

Chapter 6

1. Heschel, <u>Man's Quest for God</u>, page 111.

2. Abraham E. Millgram, <u>An Anthology of Medeviel Hebrew Literature</u>, New York:Burning Bush Press, 1961, page 194-195.

3. Heschel, <u>Man's Quest for God</u>, page 139.

4 Abraham Joshua Heschel, <u>God in Search of Man</u>, pp. 348 ff.

5. Joseph Gorfinkle, <u>The Eight Chapters of Maimonides on Ethics</u>, New York:AMS Press, 1966, page 66.

6. Theodore Weinberger, unpublished dissertation, 1991.

7. <u>Jewish Spiritual Journeys</u> Hoffman and Wolf, eds., page 173.

8. Heschel, <u>Man's Quest for God</u>, page 106.

9. <u>Magic Eye Gallery: A Showing of 88 Images</u>, Kansas City:Andrews and McMeel, 1997, pages 4, 12, and 93.

    Reprinted with permission by Magic Eye Inc., copyright 1997. For further information, refer to www.magiceye.com.

Chapter 7

1. Rabbi Dr. Charles B. Chavel, <u>Ramban: Writings and Discourses, vol. 1</u>, New York:Shilo Publishing House.

2. Saperstein, <u>Land of Israel in Pre-Modern Thought</u>, Hoffman.

3. Quoted in <u>Legends of Jerusalem</u>, by Zev Vilnay, JPS, 1973, page 205.

4 Eisen, Hoffman, page 285.

5. Translated by Rachel Rabinowitz, <u>Feast of Freedom: RA Haggadah</u>.

6. Marc Saperstein, "Land of Israel in Pre-Modern Thought," <u>The Land of Israel: Jewish Perspectives</u>, Lawrence Hoffman, ed., U of Notre Dame Press, 1986, page 219.

7. <u>Telling the Tale: A Tribute to Elie Wiesel on the Occasion of his 65th Birthday</u>, ed. Harry James Cargas, St. Louis:Time Being Books, 1993, pp. 168-169.

Chapter 8 & Conclusion

1. Martin Buber, <u>Tales of the Hasidim: Early Masters</u>, page 107.

2. "My Mystical Encounter," by Daniel C. Matt, <u>Moment</u>, February 1997, page 43.

3. Peter Berger as quoted in Theodore Weinberger.

4 Yitz Greenberg, <u>The Third Great Cycle of Jewish History</u>, published by CLAL: The National Jewish Center for Learning & Leadership.

5. Heschel, <u>Man's Quest for God</u>, page 45.

6. Sherwin, <u>Sparks Amidst the Ashes</u>,

7. Martin Buber, <u>Tales of the Hasidim: Early Masters</u>, page 173

8. By Lawrence Kushner, from <u>Honey from the Rock: An Easy Introduction to Jewish Mysticism</u>, copyright Lawrence Kushner. Woodstock, VT:Jewish Lights Publishing, 1990, pages 139-140. $14.95 pb + $3.50 s/h. Order by mail or call 800-962-4544. Permission granted by Jewish Lights Publishing, P.O. Box 237, Woodstock, VT 05091.

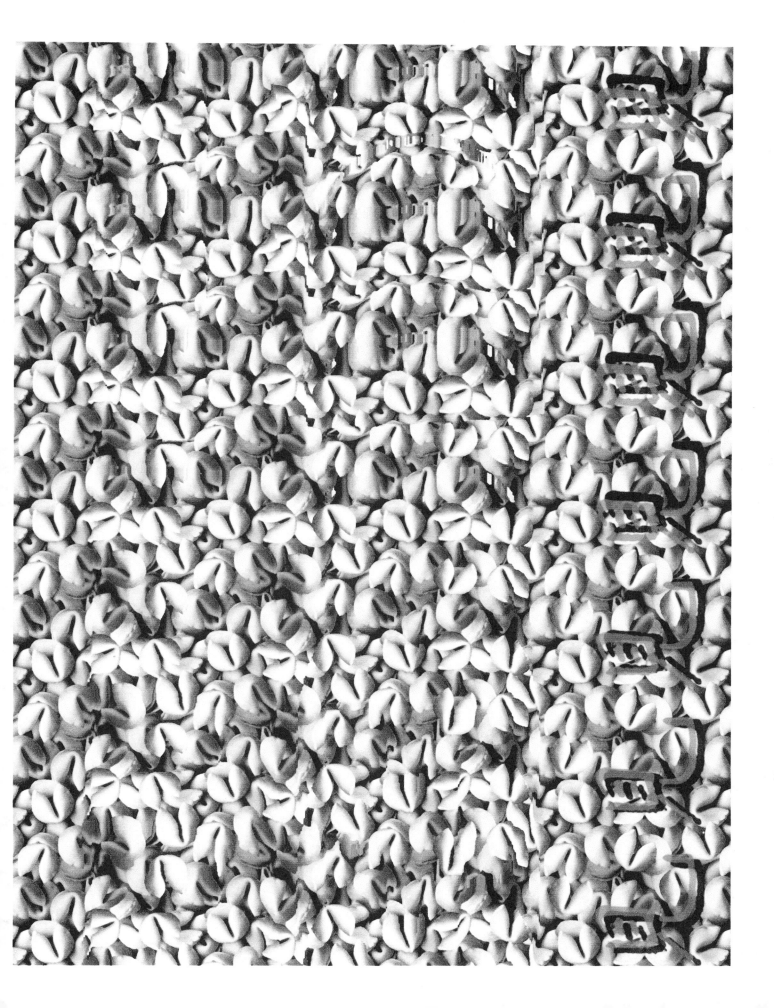

About the Author

Rabbi Nina Beth Cardin, a graduate of the Jewish Theological Seminary, is the editor of <u>Sh'ma</u> magazine, published by CLAL: the National Center for Learning and Leadership. She lives with her family in New Milford, New Jersey.